Fresh Ink

NONFICTION, FICTION, AND POETRY BY YOUNG ADULT WRITERS

Edited by Janet Nichols Lynch

iUniverse, Inc.
New York   Bloomington

iUniverse books may be ordered through booksellers or by contacting:

iUniverse
1663 Liberty Drive
Bloomington, IN 47403
www.iuniverse.com
1-800-Authors (1-800-288-4677)

ISBN: 978-1-4502-1890-0 (sc)
ISBN: 978-1-4502-1891-7 (ebook)

Printed in the United States of America

iUniverse rev. date: 03/15/2010

ACKNOWLEDGMENTS

Within these pages are the products of the 2009-2010 Creative Writing class at El Diamante High School in Visalia, California. We, the writers and editor, would like to thank our administration for its support in the publication of this anthology.

TABLE OF CONTENTS

Nonfiction

THE FROZEN PENDULUM
BY JENI CHAVEZ

THE GRAY CLOUDS BEGIN to roll, and thunder breaks free as the sky cries. It makes the playground gloomy, and the bell screams out telling us to get to class. I pull the oversized, gray, hooded sweater over my little self, making sure the rain doesn't soak my long, black hair. It covers my soft brown skin until all that's exposed are my small almond eyes.

I walk through the red door of my classroom into a warm, cozy environment. I sit down in my assigned seat and class begins. My teacher starts to talk about math, and I gaze out the window. Something wet on my hand startles me out of my trance, and I look down to see blurriness. Wiping my vision back into focus, I finish the lesson.

The day goes by, and soon enough I'm running across the muddy field to meet my daddy. I open the door to his little, gray, broken-down Honda and get in. I shiver, trying to warm up next to the roaring heater, while my daddy chuckles and drives on. We get home and settle down in front of the TV. Daddy turns on our heater made to look like a fireplace. We watch the funniest show on until the sun sets, and my mom hurries through the door, shaking off her wet umbrella. After she warms up, she begins making dinner. Around the table we laugh and eat, telling stories about things that happened that day. Soon after I help my mom clean up, we all go to bed.

I'm crying, for no reason at all really. It is the middle of the night, and my daddy must have heard me because I feel his warm embrace around my body, and his scruffy, deep voice singing to me, "You are my sunshine, my only sunshine…"

Before I know it, I am waking up the next morning,. It's 5:30. Mom walks into my room and puts a hand to my head, brushing my hair aside.

"Daddy told me you had problems sleeping last night. What's wrong?" she asks with worried eyes.

"I don't know. I've been sad for a whole week. It feels like something's wrong," I whisper.

"Well, nothing's wrong, sweetie. Cheer up, okay? Now get up and get ready. Daddy's taking you to the bus stop today."

I begin the day and get into the truck with my daddy. He begins coughing rapidly, and his whole body rumbles. He pops in a cough drop and smiles at me. My attempt to smile back fails as he drives on. We pull up to the school where my bus stop is, and he rumbles with coughing again. He gets out a breathless "Go ahead," and I quickly grab my stuff and jump out of the truck. I cross the street and stand with my friends as my daddy, smiling and waving, drives off. I begin to cry and rush into this unfamiliar school's office. I ask to use the phone and call my mom at home, hoping she hasn't gone to work yet.

"Hello?" I hear on the other line.

"M-mom? I-I think s-something's wrong w-with d-daddy," I whimper.

"What? No, no, honey. Daddy's right here. He says he's fine. He just has a sore throat. He's staying home today, okay?"

I knew it wasn't a cold he was dealing with "O-okay," I say and hang up.

I return to the bus stop just in time to get on. I get to school and try to focus on getting ready for the sixth grade culture fair. The day goes by, and I keep my tears in. After school the fair starts and my parents arrive. About an hour goes by, and my daddy mentions he's beginning to feel ill. My mom explains to my teacher that we all need to leave early, and so I say bye to my friends and go home.

When we get home, my mom has to help walk my daddy inside and into the bedroom. He falls asleep right away, and I notice that he's breathing kind of funny. His skin looks a sickening yellow color and I remember his eyes being bloodshot that day. I close the door quietly and peek around the small boxed hallway to see my mom crying on the phone. She hangs up, and I walk over to her.

"We need to go," she whispers.

Next thing I know I'm sitting in the living room of my mom's friends Paula and Bill. *How did I get here? What happened? I can't remember the drive.*

"Okay, Jeni, we're going to go to sleep now," says Paula. "If you need anything come wake me up."

As Bill hands me the remote, Paula places a blanket on my lap. They turn off the light and head for bed.

I slowly began to feel my senses coming back. The tingling in my fingertips and toes rapidly pulse. My breathing quickens as my vision returns. My stomach knots. My hearing is so strong I can hear the tick-tock of the clock hanging above the fireplace. I start to panic and become short of breath, now gasping for air. My eyes dart from side to side, looking at everything. My hands and feet become clammy as I can feel a hot shudder slither down my spine. It seems as though everything is growing tall and big, and I'm shrinking.

I close my eyes, smother my ears with my hands, and bite down hard on my bottom lip. Curling up into a ball, I hide under the blanket and stifle a tear.

No, I think. *Pull yourself together, Jeni. Daddy taught you to be stronger than this. Never cry. There's never any reason to cry. Crying is bad. Crying shows you're weak. Daddy says to be strong!*

I slowly sit up and turn on the TV, making sure it's low so I don't wake up the sleeping children in the next room. I can't seem to focus on what's on the channel, so I switch it. Click. Click. Click. Click. Click.

An advertisement channel comes on, and I watch it. It doesn't really matter to me, but I like feeling that someone is looking at me, talking to me. It makes me believe someone cares. It keeps my mind occupied, and I begin to calm down.

As one advertising ends, another begins, until they all stop, and I begin to panic again. I get up and realize I'm past the point of quivering and now beginning to shake intensely. My teeth are chattering, and my head is tingling, beginning to pound. I look up to see it's two in the morning. Only three hours have passed. I pace up and down the hall just to get moving. I'm cold, but the thermometer says otherwise.

Why couldn't Mom have just taken me to the hospital? I could be there right now instead of here, not knowing what's going on. I go and sit back down on the couch and flip through the channels once again. I settle for the news and lie down, suddenly feeling my body give up on me. I close my sore, puffy eyes, and let the blackness start to take over my vision. A single ring flows through the entire house, slicing through the dead silence.

My eyes fly open, my body gets up, and my breathing stops. I run down the hallway to Paula and Bill's room. The door is ajar, so I rush in. With big eyes, I look into their tired faces, back and forth. Paula then hangs up the phone and looks at me.

"We need to go," she whispers.

Everyone rushes to get ready and we all pile into the mini van. I space out and the next thing I remember is sitting in a Pepto-Bismol pink room with an overly clean smell in the air. Daddy lies peacefully on the bed, his scruffy facial hair grown out and his hair now wavy from sleeping. Family members all come and go. All I know is that I'm staring out the window for the longest time, not noticing anything. I do know two days have passed since that night because someone with short hair, a blurry face, and a sad voice tries to get my mom and I to go downstairs to eat and sleep. We decline every time, and I go back to the window, continuing to stare.

The third day comes, and it's around noon. I keep going in and out of the ward where my daddy is, and I keep pacing back and forth. Someone walks me to where my daddy is lying in a hospital bed and tells me to say bye.

I shake my head. "No," I whisper. "Not bye. See you later." I kiss my daddy on the forehead. I walk out and pace the halls again, wondering if anyone at school knows why I'm gone or even if they notice.

I look at a clock, and it says 5:20 PM. I walk through the doors to my dad's ward and begin walking to his room. Another small, chubby figure with a blurry face grabs my hand and walks me the other way.

We exit the doors, and she hands me to someone who I think is Paula. She gets on her knees and looks at me, tears flowing from her eyes. Her tight hug assures me of what has just happened. My breathing stops for a second, and my legs give out. I fall to the floor still in Paula's arms. Tears pour from my eyes, but I don't let out a cry. I don't know what to do, or even how to react. Blackness swallows my world, and everything numbs once more.

As my eyes open, I look around to see I'm at home in my parent's bedroom, lying next to my mom. I look at the clock. 7 AM. I walk into the living room. I see a lot of food and many family members filling up the tables and seats. I walk up to my aunt, and she turns to me, looking shocked.

"How long have I been asleep?" I mumble.

"Three days. Do you need anything?" she asks with big eyes.

"Take me to school," I state and walk away.

I get washed up and head to school. The bell rings as I get there, so I go to class. My friends Krisie and Allie know about *it*, so I wonder if word got around. The day goes by, and no one asks me questions or gives me the I'm-sorry-for-your-loss look. I start to realize something. No one really cares. No one stops his or her life to think about somebody else. The world just keeps on going. It rushes by, with its emotions and different colors, while I stand here still. Frozen in time.

MY OTHER WORLDS
BY MAREN PETERSON

Seventh Grade

I sit in history, watching the politician's debate, back and forth, back and forth. While I watch, I think of something interesting. They are at a point where one word can make or break their career. They are at a point where one word can change the future of the nation.

Their whole debate comes back down to word choice. And if they put these words in the right order they can charm the country and change the world.

The more I think about it the more I want to master the language. I feel that if I could just do that, truly master words, then I would have the world at my fingertips.

Kindergarten

my mommy says kintergarten is fun. im scared. i wak into the rom. my techer is nice. she smiles alot. we don't do alot today.

we lern are letters later. i lov how the shapes on the pag becom leters. my techer reeds to us. we sit on the big red mat on the flor. i sit in my own space and lisen.

i dont no how she finds words in the shapes. i want to do that to.

we start lerning words. the shapes turn into storees. my techer cals me over for a test. i read to her.

the bear ran to the for-est.

she says very good, you're the best reader in the class.

i smile. i leave. i feel good. i like reading. i love reading.

Third Grade

During free time I decide to read. I choose a book out of my teachers many bookcases. Its a book Ive never seen before. The cover is dark, a girl opening a door. It feels very heavy in my hand. It feels important. I sit down, and start to read.

Suddenly Im not in the classroom anymore. Im in a house, Im in pigtails, and there is a suitcase at my feet. My great-aunt comes down the stairs. "Your room is second door on the right, dinner is at six. I don't tolerate tardiness."

"Maren!"

The image fades as quickly as it had appeared. My best friend sits beside me. "I called you like five times." She says.

I try to explain what just happened, how the page became reality. How the spiky letters built a house around me. She just looked at me like I belonged in an insane asylum.

Maybe she was right.

I start to read, eager for it to happen again, but it didn't.

After I set it down, I could never find the book again.

Tenth Grade

I sit in front of the page. Pure white stares back at me. Nothing is coming to mind. Nothing has come to mind for a couple of weeks. I have the worst version of writer's block imaginable.

It scares me. I always have some idea that I can write about. My mind and pen hadn't failed me yet.

I walk away from the page, feeling disappointed. I hope that someday soon that page will be filled with my writing.

A couple of days later I find myself in church, sitting and listening. I'm not really paying attention. My mind is wandering. Then, as if a light clicked on, I think of an idea. I jot it down on the paper in front of me.

When I get home I throw myself in front of my notebook and write frantically. I fill one page, then another, then another. And it feels like a dam has been broken and water is rushing through. When I am done, about four pages are filled with my untidy scrawl. Filled with dense forests and a desperate yet desirable band of heroes.

I smile, and for days after I'm in an amazing mood. My friends ask me, "What's wrong?" I just smile mischievously and think of the page that is now full of writing.

Second Grade

Library time is my favorite time. I am careful in there, in that temple of books. I touch the spines of books as I walk pass, and I wish I could read them all. I choose the book I'll read next with care, it will become my life for the next few days.

I want to share this magic with some one. But I no no one feels the same was about books as I do.

But I no that they are missing out on alot. It is another world. They will never no. But all my worrys disapear when I open a book, and lose my self in it.

Eighth Grade

Mrs. Patton started me on poetry.
It was like the rolling sea
So many meanings could be created through the writer's woe
My understanding of literature began to grow

Limericks, sonnets, and symbols galore
I always found myself needing more
When I walked out of the class every time
I felt like I should be speaking in meter and rhyme

Fourth Grade

My teacher likes to have us write. I enjoy it. Our task is to write a nonfiction piece. I take to it with enthusiasm.

I turned in my project feeling good about it. I received a two.

It was my first grade I had ever gotten that was below proficient.

Eleventh Grade

This year I am taking Creative Writing. In the back of my head, I'm churning out ideas for my nonfiction assignment. I have a lot of ideas, but none of them are good enough.

My Calculus teacher drones on and on about derivatives. I only half-listen because I already understand it. I stare at the board that's filled with numbers.

Calculus moves to the back of my mind as I consider the idea I just had. An idea for my creative writing assignment. I cast furtive glances at my teacher while I pull on my notebook and start to write about a subject that changed my life. *Seventh Grade. I sit in history...*

Ninth Grade

I hold the phone to my ear. I can only hear static. I'm staring at my bookcase, lost in thought. The red, blue, and black spines rise and fall, making a rugged mountain terrain. Abruptly an idea occurs to me. Every book has its own world. Its own take on reality. I imagine that each book, each world has its own planet in the stars. That somewhere the characters live.

I want to create a world like that. I want to be able to have a world, inside of me, that's all my own. And put it down to paper, let others experience it. I clutch the phone to my ear, excited with all the possibilities.

"What are you doing?" Daniel, my best friend, asks.

I don't say anything for a minute. "Staring at my bookcase," I reply into the phone

"Why?"

I don't answer him. He cajoles, he pleads, so finally, I give in.

"I was thinking," I say.

"About what?" he asks.

"I want to be a writer," I say, marveling at how the words sound in my mouth. "I want to be a writer."

BELIEVING IN MIRACLES
BY MANUEL MAGAÑA

IT WAS A WARMHEARTED day in spring, eight years back. We were living in south central L.A., Home of the Angels. I was eight years old. My mother was making dinner that day while I was sitting on the couch next to my little brother Orlando, watching the news together. The day didn't seem to look like it was going to turn out to be a bad day.

In that moment "Breaking News" was displayed on the television,. "It seems there was a fight between a Hispanic male and eight African-Americans. They seem to be students from Jordan High School in south central L.A.," the news reporter said.

I thought of my brother Ivan. How could a tall, skinny, short-haired thirteen-year-old guy fight eight African-Americans, ages 15 through 17? I looked at my mother and asked, "Does Ivan go to a school called Jordan High School?"

My mom stopped chopping vegetables and looked at me as if I had told her something wrong. She hesitated, then said, "Yeah, he does. Why you ask?"

"Just wondering,," I said and looked away. Should I tell her or should I wait?

I changed the channel, but I couldn't resist the news, so I changed it back. I didn't want my mother to hear it. All of a sudden, I started getting panicky and sweaty. I started to feel the pain inside me. I was shivering. My heart was tremendously pounding. What if that Hispanic male was my brother Ivan? My eyes were shattered with tears. My eyelids began to constantly blink.

"What are you watching?" my mom asked.

I quickly changed the channel and responded, "Oh, nothing, just stupid commercials.".

"You should change the channel to the news," my mother said.

I looked away from her. My eyes must've looked like I was the kind of toy you squeeze and its eyes pop out. "The control ran out of batteries," I said.

"There are batteries in the cabinet." she said.

I walked over to the cabinet and grabbed the batteries.

"Now change to the news so that we have something to watch," my mom said.

I thought of the time when my brother Faustino was driving home from work and went through the intersection when the light turned green. The driver of a big white van, who was unfortunately talking on the phone and not paying attention, ran a red light and rammed into my brother's F-150 truck. That crash made my brother go to the hospital. Seeing my brother lying there, my mother nearly left us that day. I didn't want her to leave us now.

"Change the channel, Manuel." she said. She stopped what she was doing and walked toward the living room. The phone rang, and she walked back to the kitchen to answer it. "Hello?"

"Is this Silvia, Ivan's mother?" a lady asked.

"Yes, this is Silvia. Why, what happened?" my mom responded.

"Your son Ivan has been in a fight with other students, and he is injured," said the lady.

My mom dropped the phone, picked up her car keys, and said, "I'll be back. Watch your little brother."

"What, what happened?" I stammered.

She started crying. "Your brother. He got in a fight with eight African-Americans and they slashed him."

"Is he okay?" I asked.

She didn't respond. I started shaking. My little brother started crying. She decided to let us go with her. On our way there she could not drive because she kept thinking about my brother.

"Mom, watch out!" I screamed.

A big, lifted truck was heading toward us. Mom rapidly turned the steering wheel and stopped at the side of the road.

"Mom, let me drive. You are too stressed out to drive. Just let me drive," I said. I was just eight, but I thought I could do better than her.

"No, I'm okay," my mom said.

When we arrived at the hospital, we went from room to room looking for my brother. When we got to the right room, we saw my brother lying there. My mother started crying again. I hugged her as hard as I could.

The doctor arrived and said that thankfully Ivan was saved by a stranger on the street. "He called 911, and reported it," the doctor said.

Our family was very grateful to that stranger, the one that helped my brother out. Without him, Ivan would probably still be lying in the street. The paramedics said that they didn't see the stranger when the ambulance arrived. We will never know who he is.

The next morning my brother was well-recovered. He was just scratched by the knife that the African-Americans used to assault him. He said that when he was waiting for his girlfriend at the corner near the bus stop, eight African-Americans went up to him and started talking smack to him. "I didn't have any other choice but to defend myself and throw swings at them," he said, "but one of them was carrying a pocket knife."

"I don't know if you would still be here if it wasn't for the help of that stranger," said the doctor.

The police never arrested the guys that did this to my brother. Two weeks later, the eight African-Americans were not going to the same school as my brother. Nobody knew what had happened to them, not even the administration. They just stopped going to school.

Four weeks later, my brother dropped out of high school and began to work with our Uncle Steve. He wanted to continue going to school, but he didn't like it that much, and he said he would rather work to help the family out than go to school. He also wanted to work because he wanted to pay the hospital bill on his own, which was $8,689.

My mother said, "It doesn't matter how much the hospital bill is. What matters the most is that you are still here with us." Then again my mother started to cry. You know how mothers are. They care for their children.

It created a major impact on my life that I could have lost my brother during that conflict. Thankfully he is still with us. Two years later my other brother Faustino dropped out of high school because he also wanted to work to support the family. I was kind of melancholy, considering the fact that I wouldn't get to see my big brothers graduate. Now they admire me with every word they say because hopefully I'll be the first family member that will graduate. I will do whatever it takes to accomplish my dreams of becoming a veterinarian and to make my family proud.

I will always remember this day as the most miraculous day of my life. I am so exuberant that I still see my brother's nice smile in the morning. It inspires me to move on in life, headed in the right direction.

A NIGHT'S EVENTS
BY C. M. FRIDAY

IT WAS A SATURDAY, over a year ago, a boiling day at that, when my family and some friends ventured to the nearest water park. It was possibly one of the better days of my life considering our guests and our destination. I was quite disappointed when my friend Michael couldn't make the trip. Lucky for me, in his stead was his rather fine-looking sister and her similar-looking friend. Any other man my age would surely agree. My father was also bringing along some guests, his girlfriend Anita and her two daughters, Jessica and Sarah. My sisters were also allowed to bring guests, but the youngest didn't really have friends, which I hope will change soon, and the middle sister is just a stubborn mule who thinks that sending an invite to her friends would be a waste of time.

The day was enjoyable, and the time flew away with the sprays of water on the slides and various rides. Close to the end of the day I had to go meet my dad at the wave pool near the entrance. As he was getting out of the pool via the ladder, he slipped and hit his hip on the cement edge. When he walked out of the pool, my concern was little as we both assumed the injury would only form a bruise. Two hours later we were at my dad's house, saying goodbye to the guests. My father sent my sisters and I to our mom's house for the rest of the week.

One week later my sisters and I returned to my father's house. When he picked us up at our meeting place, he was in strange shape. His breathing was far too shallow for comfort, and he constantly gripped his left hip with a look of excruciating pain etched into his facial features. We spent the weekend in our usual routine; my sisters played on the computer or watched TV as I did various activities such as reading and taking long walks.

By Sunday night my dad's pain had intensified. My curiosity and worry were piqued so I called my mother asking if I could stay one more night. I fail to describe how surprised I was that she agreed easily. For about four hours I was playing the nurse maid to my father, who watched TV in the living room. I will not deny that the whole time I was absolutely terrified. My stomach felt as if it was pouring acid onto itself, and my head began to beat as if a thousand chimps were beating on a set of bongos. Suddenly, my dad's pain increased tenfold. I am sorry that I am unable to tell of the proceedings of the next ten minutes, for such was the state of my panic that everything happened in a dreamlike state. I only remember how it ended; my father and I got into his fancy car, and he started driving toward the hospital. All the while I could only sit in the passenger seat, one hand on the steering wheel to help steady the car as his breaths got shorter and his face more contorted.

Near a mall we were suddenly stopped by a few officers who were there because of a car crash. I saw a VW Beetle with a smashed trunk and an ambulance parked near it. Oddly enough, I was able to remember to send forth a small prayer for the victims of the accident, despite my state of panic and despair.

After a brief conversation with an officer about my father's condition, he suggested that we call our closest relatives, which at the time happened to be my grandparents on my mother's side of the family, to give us a ride to the hospital. After twenty minutes of grunts and shallow breaths from my father and silent grieving from myself, my grandparents pulled up beside our car to assist us. The plan was for my dad and me to get into my grandfather's car while my grandma followed us in my dad's car. It was a difficult process of getting my father to the other car, which required assistance from a fireman and an officer. Finally, around ten o'clock, we were off, headed toward the hospital again. The trip was silent and tormenting for me; my emotional dam finally broke, and I was unable to hide my worry. Mentally I was calling myself weak and pathetic, thinking that there was more that I could do than just sit around, offering my father the occasional comforting hand on his shoulder. I averted my eyes, fearing that he would be much more worried to see me so broken up. If ever there was a night that was my worst, it would be this one.

We finally arrived at the hospital, and everything seemed to go into fast-forward motion. We grabbed a nearby wheelchair, and my grandfather and I placed my dad in it. After a quick talk with the receptionist we were told to wait in the nearby line of chairs that made up the waiting room. I don't remember how, but I had a current issue of *Gotrek & Felix* in my hands. I opened the book to where the bookmark was and began to read. This seemed futile, as after every few words my mind drifted to other ideas, wondering how much pain was my father in, what would happen to him, and did I forget to turn off the computer or close the fridge.

Unfortunately, I wasn't able to get very far in the book before my emotional dam burst again. The anxiety was too much for me and for that I cursed myself for not being able to stand it. Tears dripped into my book, shifting letters into new shapes that interested the eye. I'll never forget what my father said to me at that moment.

From his wheelchair, he placed a hand on my shoulder and spoke through gritted teeth and ragged breaths. "It's alright. It's okay."

These four little words helped me calm down and keep my feelings in check as I waited for my father to go in to see the doctor. A heartbeat later a nurse took the handlebars of his wheelchair and pushed him into a nearby room. We were told to wait in the waiting room as the doctor worked on my dad. My grandparents and I prayed for him as we waited. I took the time to reflect on the evening's events. Soon the doctor walked up to us with news that made me one of the happiest men in the hospital. It seems that my father had torn tissues and muscles in his ribs, caused from his fall at the water park the previous weekend, but the injury was not all that serious. All he needed was painkillers and some pills to help regenerate the tissues and muscles.

The trip back to my dad's house was a total blank to me. At last I was able to finally relax and feel peace from the good news. When we arrived home, I placed my father in his bed, him smiling at me and me at him. I was about to head off to my bed when my grandmother called me from outside on the driveway, telling me I had a phone call. It was my mother. She told me to come home instantly. Confused, I asked her why. She gave me no reason. I spoke with her in a hushed fury. Why the bloody hell was she saying that I must return home when only a few hours ago she agreed wholeheartedly to let me stay? She only stated that I *must* come home. As soon as I hung up, I told my dad and he said to go, that I shouldn't get in trouble over this.

After a silent ride home in my grandmother's car I went straight to bed, without hearing my mom or my sisters say Hello or How is dad? In some strange way my rage was slowly replaced with melancholy. Although my perspective on life didn't change suddenly, such as what happens in other tales of a similar nature, it did change gradually over time and through much reflection. I suppose I learned a few lessons that night. One would be that good health can be snuffed out in an instant, and now I understand that emotionally and not just intellectually. Another lesson would be realizing the callousness of some people and the lack of logic I'd have to deal with for a long, long time.

ADDICTION
BY CHANSE SOUZA

THE LUNCH BELL RANG, and it was time for Spanish class with Mr. Mayberry. I had just split an 80 mg Oxy with my close friend Eugene, and I was already feeling good, despite the constant aches in my body. I knew what I wanted. Oxy just didn't seem like enough anymore. I wasn't numb enough. I wasn't sane enough. I wasn't hollow enough. I could still feel emotion, and I didn't want it. I was so close to being a happy robot. My body quivered. My mind was racing, and I wanted to reach into my pocket and just pop the little white pill. But I couldn't, not yet.

I sat down at my desk. It was really close to Mayberry's, adjacent to his, no more than two feet away. My desk was one of those kinds where the seat is welded to it, so there's no room to move around comfortably. I stared at the way the grain of the wood moved. It was so exquisite. I traced my finger along a wild and spontaneous dark line. I could relate to that brilliant line. It was so unique, so full of life, yet here it was, trapped in this little space with no room to continue on with its dazzling movement. I knew all too well what it is like to be contained in a small place, when everything seems to be crashing down around you, and you have no room to branch out.

There were times when I asked myself if I could really be insane. If I could be qualified enough to be strapped to a bed and constantly sedated. I don't know, but it sounded nice. As numb as I may have been, I constantly felt a knot of malice and hate swell up in my throat, waiting to be vomited out, especially when I'd hear my mother complain about my father not paying his child support. But I hated puking, and so the malevolence lived and reproduced inside me. If it wasn't for my daily dose of sanity, it wouldn't be a surprise if I had a sudden outburst of violence on some random person who was in the wrong place at the wrong time. So I chose my sanity of the

17

day: Xanax, Somas, Methadone, Oxycontin, but these were only my second choices. Sometimes, if I had the money, or batted my eyes and sashayed my hips at an all-too-willing dealer, I could have whatever I wanted. And I never denied a pill given to me. Life seemed so wrong to me. I had to grow up quick when I was pulled into the middle of my parents' vicious custody battle at the end of sixth grade, and then I lost my stepmother whom I would seek comfort from, due to her divorcing my father. I had no one to turn to for help since my parents constantly fed me their hate for each other, but I found the answer to my problems at the beginning of sophomore year, and when I snorted whatever pills I had, my life was perfect.

The late bell rang, and the last of my classmates had rushed through the door and found their seats. Mr. Mayberry stood at his podium at the front of the room and greeted us. I looked at him with half-open, heavy eyes and laughed. He was of average height, and nicely built for a man in his forties. He wore those dark-rimmed glasses that made his dark eyes look beady and gave them a sort of twinkle you'd expect to see from Santa Claus. The hair on top of his head was missing, but nothing one of those Jewish caps couldn't cover. It wasn't so much his Jewish Santa Claus appearance that made me laugh, but how he presented himself. Whenever I saw him he always seemed so giddy, like a schoolboy happy to be on a field trip.

The class took out the textbook and began working on the assignment written on the board. There was a sudden, fierce stabbing pain in the side of my head, and I winced, gritting my teeth. It subsided after a minute and reminded me what my body was longing for. The lust for the little white pill in my pocket was becoming unbearable. I needed it, and it needed me. Mayberry was busy at the front of the room conversing with a student, and it made me wonder how much teachers really care about their students. How aware was he of my life? Hah. He knew nothing. It's better that way, for everyone to be ignorant. I used to think I'd like to be ignorant. Maybe then I could stoop to the level of those I hate, and serve them the cruelty they so rightfully deserved.

It was winter, and I was forced to live in Bakersfield where it never snows, only rains. I'm not a person you would expect to complain about rain. I could watch it for hours as it would dance itself to the ground, only to become a mirror that shows me the blurry reflection of my face. That's all my life had become. One huge blur of hate, fear, lust, and trouble. Have you ever taken the time to listen to the rain sing? I have. It's quite an intriguing song. Dull, yet fierce, but it never sings alone; there is always the presence of the birds. I've always envied the birds, being able to fly and escape the world. I would want to be reincarnated as a bird, something unique and not so common, something like a golden eagle. They are so beautiful, especially when they mate with their lifelong partner. The couple will lock talons high in the air and spiral down until the deed is done. There are some pairs, however, that fall to their deaths. It makes me wonder how much I would risk for love. I would want to die that way, in the hands of my lover, knowing we would die together.

A quick look at Mayberry told me that he would be busy at his computer for awhile. I smiled, and my eager hand rushed for my pocket to finger my sanity. I couldn't bear it any longer! I took my little friend and placed it discreetly by my book. I reached for my student ID card and placed it on my desk as well. My heart was pounding against my chest. I knew the drugs were making me weak, and it wouldn't have surprised me if my heart thrust its way from its holding cell. My mind was focused on my sanity sitting before me, caressed by the sporadic lines of the desk. The yearn for my sanity grew stronger by the millisecond, and my body was becoming oblivious to its aches due to the adrenaline that was coursing through my blood.

I nudged my notebook further up the desk so I could prepare myself for bliss. I propped up my Spanish book to shield my actions from Mayberry's beady Santa Claus eyes. My fingers were quivering with excitement as I picked up my student ID. My picture disgusted me. I disgusted me. As I began to grind my sympathizer into powder, I could feel the stares. What people thought of me didn't matter; let them watch me become sane again. I finished grinding my pill, scraping the last chunks off my ID card. The innocent white powder was so damn beautiful. Nothing made me happier than my powdered love before me. I collected all the dust I could and shaped it into a single thin line. My nose began to tingle with excitement. I knew all too well what was coming. I quickly retrieved my handy dandy rolled dollar bill, and smelled its crisp scent. The stares grew more intense, and I could feel them honing in on my target. I put the bill to my left nostril, placed a finger on my right, and inhaled my powdered sanity. That's what I liked about winter; it was easier to cover up the sniffles since everyone had them. It disgusted me in a way. I wanted to tell people to blow their noses. But what can you expect when you live in a land of filth?

I sat back in my seat, stretched my legs in front of me, closed my heavy eyes and grinned. My nose burned, and there was a pain in my head again. I welcomed the sting. It was a reminder I was still alive and now sane. My hands fell to my sides, and I could feel my friend at work in my body. It made my veins dance convulsively, it made my pounding heart slow its pace, and my mind was now at ease. I could hear my blood flowing, carrying with it my sanity. This feeling is something I can never forget.

The blond next to me, Alexis, asked in her whiny high-pitched voice, "Did you really just snort that?" This stupid, stuck up cheerleader irked me.

"Yes."

"Oh my God, you're crazy! What did you just snort?"

Maybe I am crazy? I wouldn't know. I did know that I just railed the best damn thing man has created. I turned my head and looked her in the eyes.

"Morphine."

She shook her big, overly-dyed head and continued working. I sat at my desk, enveloped in bliss. The morphine was coursing through my veins, and I never wanted it to stop, not only because of how good it felt, but because of the pain it brought when the high was over. Smoking marijuana helped with the pain, but nothing could cure it like another dose of morphine.

There came a time shortly after this day, where I had to learn to deal with the pain. The drama with my parents hadn't ceased, and it pushed me to use even more, making my life at home even more miserable. My mother had found my stash of pot and decided I was a danger to my younger brother and sister. She only knew about the pot. I most likely would've been sent to rehab if she and my stepfather knew about all the other drugs. If they only knew what it was like to be an addict.

My mother decided to give up her child support and send me to live with my father, who was thrilled about not having to pay the child support. My move to Visalia finally gave me a reason to get clean, even though I was constantly fighting with myself. The deal with my parents was that I had to stay clean or get shipped off to rehab. My body would convulse and yearn for its fix. The continuous aches and pains withdrawal gave me made me feel as if I had been hit by a bus, run over by a train, and stabbed by long, cruel knives in every inch of my body. I burned, I twitched, I screamed in agony, and I sweat until I thought there wasn't an ounce of fluid left in me. I knew I couldn't let anyone see me like this; they wouldn't understand.

I kept it quiet and went to school in constant pain. The chills came and went, and my body was exhausted from shivering. I didn't like to vomit, but I couldn't help it one day when I got back from school. There were times I cried for so long, I thought I would permanently see blurs. Death seemed kind, but I was too much of a coward to die alone. That made me think, would anyone really miss me if I was gone? I had no one to love me. There was no one to save me from myself.

I was the only one who saved me. It was through willpower. My will to get clean for those who needed me, and for myself. I knew there was more to life than the hell I was put through. I wanted to prove to those who doubted me that they were wrong. I am no longer the failure they thought I was.

During my withdrawal, and because of the insomnia, I had too much time to think about my drugs. At times, I felt my sanity slipping from me again. I needed my drugs. I yearned for them every day, but I had to prove to myself that I could be somebody. It hurt me physically and mentally to give up what made me so happy. I locked it all away, my addiction, my pain, but even today, I find there's always that itch in the back of my mind, to use again.

Fiction

YOU'LL SEE MY FACE
BY LILY THAO

"**M**ARY ALICE, CAN YOU hand me the tape gun?"

"No, Kara, I can't. I'm too busy thinking of ways to die."

"I swear, Mary Alice! Cut it out with the sarcasm, yeah?"

Kara is my mom, but I disowned her last month when she broke the news that we are moving from Maine to sunny California. Yea! Not. So now she's just Kara. Kara wants us to move in with some guy named Craig from Los Angeles. Okay, when a man asks you to move in after nine months of on-line dating, it just screams creep incognito. There is just something about the way he puffs out his chest that is embroidered with curly, black hair, then strokes his beard, saying, "Kara, your beauty is my demise." It is disgustingly creepy. All the guys she ever dates are either balding or have massive body hair. She can do so much better considering every boy I bring home falls in love with her rather than me. I don't blame them. Kara has these gorgeous, deep blue eyes, wavy, blond hair that ripples in the wind, and a body of a goddess. Curves and breasts. I'm just a sixteen-year-old girl who hasn't filled in her body yet and never will. All I have are braces and brown-colored eyes. There's hoots and whistles when she passes by and silence when I do.

But whatever Kara wants, Kara gets. That's how it's always been. Like the time I was eleven and I wanted to be a princess for Halloween, but Kara wrapped me in tin foil and said that I was a baked potato. So I'm stuck here in this dusty, old attic trying to pick up lost memories and package them into boxes.

"Tape gun, Mary Alice."

I ignore Kara, and she throws a shoe at me. "Honestly, kid, you're not going to die from moving, so suck it up! Craig is a really nice guy. He…"

25

Her voice fades away as my mind wanders into some other place that does not include her.

Picture albums, knickknacks, and baby clothes all in one box. Fold the box and then seal it with tape. Same old, same old. I'm getting sick and tired of this attic. It smells like rusty pipes and cat poop, or like a wet towel that never dried.

"...has money, Mary Alice. You know how tight of a budget we're on these days."

Money, money, money is all she ever talks about. It is as if we have none or not enough to survive. Her single-mom earnings from the diner and my pitch-ins from working at the roller rink is enough, but with Kara enough is never enough.

"...so please be understanding, hun."

I wish she would just shut up. I get up and walk through the dark, dusty attic towards the very back. Maybe then I can block her from my mind.

I stumble on who-knows-what beneath me. Through the tiny window is a ray of light shining in so I can see tiny dust particles float in the air. The sun beams its rays onto a wooden chest. The top is carved with intricate mermaids and waves. The latch is gold, and it sparkles and gleams in the light. Wiping away years worth of dust, I run my hands over it like it was a child, caressing it eagerly, but softly. I trace the designs with my fingers, moving through the ripples on the wood.

Carved in the corner of the lid is Kara's great-grandmother's name, Agnes Gwendolyn Prince. I remember, now. This chest was given by my great-great-grandmother to Nana's mom, to Nana, and finally to Kara. It is a chest passed down from a mother to her daughter when she gets married.

I know I shouldn't dig into Mom's things, but the mermaids are calling me with their lovely voices. I unlatch it and lift the lid, revealing items galore. Kara's veil. The white lace is soft on my fingertips. I can just imagine her walking down the isle toward Dad, and he is handsome with his topaz eyes and light brown hair. Old movie tickets: *Superman*. Dad told me it was the movie where he kissed Kara the first time. After that they began "going steady" as he called it. Memories all packed into one wooden box: love letters, wedding bands, photos, and a receipt from Oceanside Diner, Kara's work place since she was sixteen. That was where Dad first met her. He said he had never seen a girl serve crab cakes as cute as she did, and he fell in love with her the moment she slipped and fell on orange juice.

I don't know why she's kept these things all these years, even after Dad left. They loved each other, I know it. But who knows what happened between them ten years ago? I sure don't have a clue. Continuing my rampage through the box, I pull out more keepsakes, one by one, admiring each piece of the puzzle. I finally reach the bottom, not to find Kara's or Dad's properties, but mine. It's my boomerang, the one Dad gave me ten years ago at Gold Beach before he left me. A knot builds in my chest like I am choking on my heart while it is still pulsing.

Chiming laughter fills my head and a little girl's voice like a recording begins to play, "Row, row, row, your boat, gently down the stream...Lemme try, Daddy!... No, you can't go. Who's gonna make the monsters be nice to me?"

Warm, salty tears collect on my lips. I remember. Dad disowned me ten years ago as I did Kara a month ago. What would he call me now? I'm no longer Mary Alice or his daughter. Would he call me kid? Girl? You?

The boomerang in my hands is like holding a bit of love, just like Dad said it was ten years ago.

"Mary Alice, do you see this boomerang?" he asked

"Yes, Daddy!"

"Well, it is like love. No matter how far you throw it, with no matter how much strength you use, and no matter how far it would like to go, it always comes right back to the same place it left."

He lied to me. He was *my* love, so then why has he not returned to me after these ten years? Each year that I waited, I became bitter and more bitter, until the bitterness drowned my heavy heart into its sea. Somewhere out there in the sea, my heart travels, hunting for Dad, but as for me, I refuse to search for him.

All I have ever wanted was my Dad. I hated Father's Day after he left. At school we would always make those stupid magnets with our pictures and thumb print on it as gifts. I had no one to give it to, so every year I would hide it underneath my bed, saving each one for when Dad would come home. I especially hated "Breakfast for Dads." Seeing all those girls with their dads made me so jealous. They giggled as their dads would lift them up and swing them around and around. Their dads would kiss their little noses when they cried. They held hands when they walked on with their lives. And me, I always sat outside looking in at all the love that I would never have. Every year was the same. "Mary Alice, where is your dad, honey?" I looked up at my teacher with my little brown eyes that sat in tears.

"I don't have one," I answered shamefully.

"Everyone has a dad, my dear."

"No, not everyone."

I look at the boomerang in my hands. My knuckles turn white as I squeeze tighter and tighter. I want all those images of my dad and all those memories of not having him to leave me alone.

"Honey?"

"Yeah, Kara?"

"What's that you have in your hand?"

"Nothing."

"Give it."

I place the boomerang in her hands. She looks at it with her soft, blue eyes and touches her lips. She looks from me to the boomerang and back to me. Next thing I know I am cradled in her arms and here I go. Once hung up so high, my thread is broken and I'm falling faster and faster. Sobs and tears choke me as I tremble in the light that the tiny window lets in. Mom joins me in the fall from sanity, and we both sit in the light and cry.

After minutes that feel like hours, she lets me go. She moves toward the chest and digs through it as if she has lost something. She pulls out an envelope. It's white but discolored, probably from the years it has been locked up in this old attic. She places it on my lap and walks away. On the envelope is written my name, "Mary Alice Agnes Jones." I lift the tab and pull out what seems to be a letter. I read

> August 26, 1999
> Traveler of the great roads of life,
> Everyday feels a little closer to where it is that you're
> headed for, given a hope of so much more in life. Think
> you're on this road alone? Looking for a truth that is
> untold? Many times you've been close to breaking, giving
> up, and letting go. Your heart says it's not over. For every
> time you break into tiny shards, just remember there will
> be a lighted soul to guide your journey. But if you choose
> to turn away, there in the mirror, in the reflection, you'll
> see my face. And when the world begins to crowd your
> space, remember days when noise was silenced. No more
> empty vows, no loveless displays, just a sense of knowing
> you'll see my face.

"What Kara?! What?! Before what? Before he left?!" My voice echoes to the rafters, scaring me with its power.

"Before he died! He died, Mary Alice! When are you going to accept it?"

The word "died" seeps slowly into my skin like acid rain burning me slowly. How could this be? He couldn't have died. Never. Lies. All lies.

"When are you going to end these games with yourself? It's not healthy! He is dead! It's been that way for ten damn years. Why do you keep lying to yourself?"

"No, you're the liar! He left us because we weren't good enough."

"He had pancreatic cancer! That's why he left us. It's not what you've allowed yourself to believe."

"You're a liar! He never died, *you liar!*" I pick up odds and ends from the floor and begin to throw them at Kara. I don't know how tears become an hysterical cry, but they do. My fall has ended and now my feet are touching the peak of crazy. Kara stands still, makeup smearing her face, allowing me to hit her with everything I can get my hands on. I pick up the boomerang and prepare to throw it, but it slips from my hand in defeat, hitting the floor with a light thud.

Pancreatic cancer. I remember that day sitting outside of his hospital room.

"Well , Mr. Johnson, I am sorry to say that you have only days, maybe a few weeks at the most," the doctor told him.

"To live?" he whispered lightly, for he knew that I sat outside the door.

"Yes, I am very sorry."

And the day of the funeral, when people said, "I am sorry for your loss, Mary Alice," I remember replying, "I didn't lose anything. I think he lost me."

"Oh, poor thing," some old lady whispered, "she doesn't understand a thing."

But I did understand. I just refused to accept the understanding. I wanted him to be alive so badly that I made up stories in my mind to keep him alive, even if it meant that I hated him for the past ten years. So every truth, I tied with a lie-coated ribbon. Every pain, I painted black with hate. But now, now the ribbons have been untied. The black paint chipped off the pain, leaving it bare and raw. The truth is now exposed.

I pick up the letter and finish the last bit.

> And in my face you'll see, a tiny light, shining innocence.
> A part of love that got away, that is now returning. So
> no matter how far away I am, there in the mirror, in the
> reflection, you'll see my face. I love you, Mary Alice.
>
> Love, Dad

P.S. I am like the boomerang. No matter how far I may go, no matter how long I am gone, I always come right back to the same place I left.

Mom picks up the boomerang and embraces it as if it were her lover, then she motions it toward me. Her wet eyes are pleading me to except it. I take it from her into my own hands. I hold it up to the sunlight, arm stretched toward the window. In the tiny light, shining of innocence, the boomerang reflects a part of love that got away, but has now returned.

ALL WE HAVE
BY JENNA PARMLEY

D AVID WALKED DOWN THE small streets of the French town *Cordes-sur-ciel*. The paths were busy as people walked around from place to place, living their daily lives. The rain had let up for the moment, but the slick stones and puddles, though reflecting the little sunlight there was, seemed to make the city gloomy and cold. No one hurrying by smiled, and only rarely did they stop to talk.

David himself embodied the gloomy attitude of the town. His wet, shoulder length, brown hair was tied back in a ribbon, and his breeches were torn and patched. His shirt did not look new, but it was clean. His eyes were troubled as he read the paper in his hands. He hurried on along the street, and his eyes raced just as fast, taking in the words. He sighed at it, frustrated, and folding it, shoved it in his pocket.

His pace didn't slow as he turned a corner. He passed the small community church and looked to see a family in the graveyard just past it. They stood around a coffin only two or three feet long. David slowed just a bit as he offered a prayer for the family, but he took off again, and as soon as he turned the next corner, he forgot all about them.

He had almost reached his destination when he heard his name from behind him. It was his friend Leo, running up the street. Leo looked very much like David, though his hair was a lighter shade.

"David, I've been looking for you. Boss told me to let you know that he didn't need us today."

David sighed and shook his head. This was not good. How was he ever going to earn the money he needed if one of his jobs fell through? He shook his head as he thought of the Queen, Marie Antoinette. She spent more money in a day than he'd make in his whole life. The folded bill in his pocket seemed to gain weight as he went over the numbers in his head. Leo broke into his reverie.

"I went to your house to look for you first and told Elise. She wanted me to tell you that if you had nothing else to do you could go home and help her with some of the projects."

"Yes, I should go help." They started walking back up the street. David turned to Leo. "What are you doing right now?"

"I don't have work either, and your lovely sister said I could come back with you and help."

David smiled and couldn't resist teasing Leo about him and "lovely" Elise. They walked past the church again, this time not even seeing the funeral.

They reached the edge of the shops of the town and walked through the little rows of houses. Just before the edge of the trees was a small, two-room house. Out front was a beautiful girl with a long, brown braid falling down her back. Her dress was threadbare with patches and streaks of dirt covering it. She smiled when she saw the two men coming toward her.

"David, I'm glad you came. Charlie is in the trees, and he says he wants to show us something. Leo, will you go ahead? Charlie wanted your help."

Leo nodded and headed off to help David and Elise's little brother, and they followed at a slower pace.

"Elise, my boss didn't need me again in work today. I don't know how we're going to pay for everything we need. I'm really worried that I'm going to lose the job."

"David, you have to promise me that you won't tell anyone I told you this." He nodded, confused. "Leo asked your boss to let you off for the day."

"What? Why would he do that?"

"Charlie and I asked him to." He looked at her still confused. "David, do you know what today is?" He continued to look at her and shook his head. "It's your birthday, hon. You're twenty-one now." David was shocked. He thought back and realized she was right.

"That doesn't mean you should take me out of work! We're never going to make ends meet! I'm going to go ask if I can work today anyway." He turned around and started walking back toward town. Elise grabbed his arm.

"Don't you dare go anywhere, David! Charlie has been working very hard on this. He and Leo and Josh have been taking extra odd jobs for the last month to raise money for a present, and everyone else chipped in as well."

"Elise, we don't have time for fun anymore. There's not enough money in the entire country, let alone this little town, to get everything we need, to get everything Charlie needs. We have nothing, Elise."

"You're wrong. We have Charlie, even if he's all we have." She started to say more but she broke into a hacking cough and only barely caught herself against a tree as she started to fall. David slid an arm around her to give support and looked at her, worried. He was silent until the coughing stopped. He pulled her into a hug after wiping a tear off her face. He whispered into her hair.

"Why didn't you tell me you had Mama's cough? How long have you had it?"

She looked at him, saying nothing. He could see the tracks the tears had left through the dirt on her face. She worked so hard for him and Charlie. He realized how much he needed her. He whispered again, almost silently, "How long?"

She answered hesitantly. "Almost three weeks."

David drew a breath. Their mother had died after five weeks of the cough. His brain raced as he tried to find solution, but he knew there was none. The doctor would cost too much, and Elise would want him to not make a fuss over her, but do everything for Charlie. His throat caught; she was going to die. She nodded as if hearing his thoughts.

"I know," she said, "but it's okay. I'll get to be with Mama and Papa, Aunt Lynn, Cousin Will, Liz, and Marie. You'll be able to buy more for Charlie, and, and…"

She stopped for a minute. David was still in shock.

"David, you have to come to this party. I know you won't do it for Charlie, since working would help him more, and you won't do it for your friends. Heaven knows that you won't do it for yourself, but please do it for me." She smiled slightly. "I need a few good stories to share when I see everyone again."

He smiled too as she mentioned this reference to one of their childhood jokes. He looked at her carefully and, still smiling a bit, he nodded. They resumed their walk through the trees, and Elise reminded David to act surprised. They came to a clearing and all their friends jumped up with a great "Surprise!"

Leo, Josh, and Charlie smiled hugely and were the first to pull David into a group hug. The rest of Leo and Josh's families were there, and some of David's work friends had come with their families. Elise's friends had come, and Charlie had one or two friends as well. They all stood around a large sheet lying on the grass that was covered with a strange assortment of foods. David could tell that each family had just brought whatever they were having for dinner that night, and had added it to the pile. It wasn't a lot, but it showed how much they all cared.

They spent the night talking and swapping stories. David had a great time, and for a few moments, forgot to be grim. About two hours after he had arrived, Charlie and Josh presented the present from everyone to him. Their twelve-year-old faces broke into identical grins as he unfolded the blanket that served as wrapping. He was excited about the new hat as his old one had finally fallen apart. He put it on immediately and smiled at the happy looks on Josh and Charlie's faces.

Elise sat off to the side and smiled the whole time. She coughed again and covered her mouth with her hand to muffle the sound. She pulled it away to find blood dripping down her palm. She silently prayed that everyone would be okay once she was gone. They were all fighters, strong and always ready, so she knew they'd make the best with the difficult situations they were given.

David felt his heart torn in half a week later when he saw her pale, lifeless face in death. Eighteen was too early to leave life. He looked around the gloomy world and smiled through the tears, knowing she had to be in a better place, a happier place.

Karsten walked down the same small streets of the French town *Cordes-sur-ciel*. The paths were busy as people walked around from place to place, living their daily lives. He passed the small church as he did every morning, and stepped into the small graveyard. He carried a flower which he laid on his cousin's grave. He stood there for a moment, remembering Liana's life, and then he turned to go.

Just before leaving the gate, he stopped to listen. He could hear singing. He looked around and realized he had not seen the man sitting by one of the newer graves. The man had shoulder length, brown hair that was tied back in a ribbon. His breeches were old and quite patched. He was holding a flower in his hand and singing quietly to the headstone. Karsten edged closer, quite a bit curious to see what one would sing to a grave. He came up from behind; the man stopped the song and began to speak.

"My dear Elise, are you with Mama? Have you told her all our stories?" He sighed. "I miss you. Charlie misses you. He's eating again though, so it's progress. I told him you were an angel now, and in a happier place, and he really liked that." He was silent for a second, but then continued. "You were wrong you know. Granted, you were a lot closer to the mark than I was, and I'm sorry it took your death for me to see that. You said Charlie was all I had left."

Karsten walked away, bored by the endless talking. He walked out the gate and headed towards his workplace. What was the world coming to? Since when did people talk with angels and sing to stones instead of working? Didn't that man know there was work to be done and money to be made?

Karsten shook his head at the lazy way of some people and as soon as he rounded the corner, he forgot all about the man, his thoughts focusing back on his own life.

In the churchyard, David finished his thought. "You were wrong." He looked down at the hat lying in his lap as he continued, "I have so much more."

THE PHONE CALL
BY MAREN PETERSON

It falls down
    Gracefully, gently
    Pounding
As though nothing is wrong
With the world
Even though
    Everything *is*
It falls like the sound of a note
    Quietly
    And small
The pitter-patter of drops
    A minor melody
The last drop
Never falls

Fact: Last night at exactly 2:20 AM I got a phone call from my friend Andy. I ignored it and went back to sleep.

Fact: The High School Grapevine says that his girlfriend broke up with him a week ago.

Fact: Regardless of Andy's trouble, I'm having a really good day today.

I walk into school, and I'm a ship floating on the water. I had a date last night, and this guy was better than all the rest of them.

Today is just good, I can feel it, and it's like my ship floats even lighter.

Fact: At exactly 8:12 I hear the worst possible news.

Andy committed suicide last night.

Right after he tried to call me. My ship suddenly and rapidly capsizes, and I'm falling, I can't breathe. The sunlight is drifting away; water clogs my throat and mouth. I drown. Water falls on my face. I look up; it's raining.

Faces float around me, and I feel like I'm turning in a circle, all the people turning into a blur, and I can't stop spinning. I find myself in last period, staring out the window, at the rain. I wonder how I got here.

Fact: Andy is dead.

Fact: I could have stopped it.

That's what the phone call was, my one chance to save my friend, my distant friend whom I had shared some good laughs with, whom I'd shared my first kiss with, whom I had first loved. But I had ignored the phone call.

Suddenly, I'm on my porch, and my chocolate lab is nosing at my hand, trying to get me to pet her. She smells like wet dog. That's because it's raining still. I wave away her nose.

The drops fall, one by one, and it's hypnotic. The rain hammers the dirt, and transforms it into mud. A conniving monster, just waiting to suck in a shoe.

Drip, drop.

I could have saved him. Drip, drop. It's all my fault. Drip drip drip. The rain won't stop, neither will my conscience.

I'm rocking back and forth; it feels like my soul is being ripped apart, I wonder if this is what it feels like to commit murder.

Because that's what I have done.

I murdered my friend by not picking up my phone.

Drop drip.

The rain won't stop.

Finally, I can't stand it anymore. I run inside and up into my room. The rain follows me. I can hear it on the roof now.

I'm scared of it.

I'm scared the rain won't stop; I'm scared I will never be able to escape this sound. Drop, drip, drop.

Drop drop drop.

I burrow under my covers. I can still hear it.

My hands grasp at the covers. They twist them, mutilate them. The rain hasn't stopped yet, and I begin to think it never will. Somewhere in the middle of this I fall asleep.

I don't know how, but when I wake up my phone is ringing, I answer it.

"It's you," Andy says. "You killed me."

I sit up screaming. My hands rip at the covers and the walls. Blood comes out from under my fingernails.

I CAN STILL HEAR THE RAIN!

It won't stop; the rain won't stop. Drip drop drop drip. I could have saved him. I could have saved him.

I sit in front of a shrink.

"Tell me what happened with your friend."

I say nothing; in my head I am screaming. I am screaming that he called me, and if I had picked up, then he might be alive right now; he might even be happy.

My fingers twist the sweatshirt in my lap. I nervously look around the room. I can't focus on a single thing.

I see the rain out the windows.

"The rain won't stop," I whisper.

"You're in Washington, dear. You can't avoid the rain," the psychiatrist says kindly.

I see myself in a mirror on the wall. My hair looks greasy. There are dark spots underneath my eyes, and my cheeks are sunken in. My eyes are completely wild.

This kind person in front of me can't help. Because there is one problem:

Fact: The rain won't stop.

CAMP OF DEMONS
BY C.M. FRIDAY

T HE BALDING MAN IN an American uniform flips the switch on the lamp
lights. A young man sits in a chair, the light glaring straight into his face.
The boy squints, wondering why he was brought to such a place. He wonders
if he is in his village, or if he is even in what was left of Pakistan at all. As his
mind wanders with unanswered questions, the aged man sits at the other side
of the table, looking at a document and sighing heavily. He says something
into a box-like device and hits a button. The box speaks in perfect Urdu, if
not a little mechanically.

"Do not worry. What is your name?" asks the little device, no bigger
than a soup bowl.

"Khurram. Why am I here?" the boy asks.

The box translates.

The man leans over the table again, and without taking his eyes off
Khurram, he speaks into the box. "Tell us how you ended up in the Imperial
Cathay Army Research Facility and what you saw there."

Khurram blinks and looks down, seeing his reflection on the table. A
boy of sixteen, matted and dirty hair, and an emaciated, scarred face. He
shakes his head, and leaning toward the translating box, he begins, "It was
four months ago, back when the I.C.A. just started its occupation of Eastern
Pakistan, after they took absolute control over the former Indian Republic.
Our village was one of the first ones to be garrisoned. An officer gathered all
of the villagers into the nearest field so that we could all 'witness the glorious
liberation from false gods and embrace the mother nation.'

"He said that we were all to be moved into an established internment
camp that was only twenty miles away from where we stood. People refused.
People were shot. My brother was shot. After that we all cooperated. We were

39

not even allowed to go back to our homes to gather any belongings. I could hear the mothers crying, unable to go back and get their babies. I am not ashamed to say I was scared and anxious.

"We were gathered into trucks that seemed to come from the Third World War. At first I wondered why they were using twenty-year-old trucks, but those thoughts disappeared when a soldier prodded me with his bayonet. I sat next to my mother and father; both were quiet and sullen from my brother's death. I did not wish to disturb them. I was depressed, too.

"I cannot tell you how long it took to get there, or what we saw on the way. My head was spinning from the rapid change of events. The death of my brother, the taking of our homes, and the forceful evacuation. When we arrived we were herded out of the trucks and onto a dirt path inside the camp like cattle to the slaughter.

"The camp was not very big, maybe about one square mile. There were many buildings; most of them were tube-like huts made of sheet metal, called barracks. At the far end of the camp was a flat, one-story building with guards walking around its walls and along its roof. Twenty people were to go into each barrack and there were forty, maybe fifty in all. No one resisted after what they had seen in the field. Soldiers prodded our backs with rifles and shotguns and yelled at us to get moving. I saw the weak and elderly shot on the spot for not being able to keep up. I even saw someone shot for helping a man who tripped. The one who tripped was shot as well.

"After that, it was everyone for themselves. Even the mothers seem to have lost most of their maternal instincts. I wanted to cry, but I thought that if I was seen crying, I would be shot too, so I kept silent, and let my heart grieve in silence.

"In assigning us to barracks, I don't think they even tried to separate us in an orderly fashion; they just gave us a bunk and we sat there. I don't know where my mother and father went. I still don't know if they are alive.

"After the first month we became really gaunt, even though we were skinny before. We were served only one meal a day. It couldn't even be called a meal; it was only two cans of beans or peas per hut. Two cans for twenty people, one can for ten people. It is a wonder we did not all die of starvation. We had to hunt rats and whatever else was edible to survive. I thought that is what the army of China, or Cathay, as they renamed themselves, wanted us to do, just die out. But then, why did they not just shoot us all?

"After the third month, rumors spread. Everyone knew that the soldiers plucked one person at random from a barrack every few days. Nobody knew what happened to these people. Some say they were target practice, and the more vulgar said they were 'toys.' All we did know is that there was an odd smell two or three days after someone was chosen. It reminded me of sweet peaches and rancid meat left in the sun. Whenever that disgusting smell came up, we saw soldiers wear gas masks over their noses and mouths. We all thought we were going to die of poison. But after a while, when nothing happened, we just learned to cope with the odor as best as we could.

"People began to get nastier. In my own barrack two men fought over a half-decayed rat. One man took a thin linen sheet that served as our blankets and used it to choke the other to death. A soldier who walked nearby heard the commotion and shot the remaining man. Afterward, we began to see soldiers more heavily equipped, and always wearing their strange leather masks. Those masks reminded me of a *rakshasa*, a cannibalistic demon that shape shifts between the face of a fierce tiger and that of an angry man. The mask's mouthpiece seemed to growl and the crude stitching contorted the wearer's features.

"More and more fights broke out the camp. Four or five people died a week. Soon, there were only about half the people alive that used to live in my village. People were short tempered and paranoid. I was like that too, but not as extreme as some others. Near the end of our second month there I was chosen to be taken away. I was scared. I wanted to reappear afterward and not just vanish like the others. I lashed out and tried to hold myself against the door jamb, but a soldier hit me with the butt of his rifle.

"I do not know how long I was unconscious, and I do not know where in the camp I was, if I was even still in the camp. I could hear things, but I kept my eyes closed. I felt myself tossed into a room, and that is when I opened my eyes. I looked around to see others in a glass room, and beyond the glass were not Chinese soldiers, but some sort of scientists. They wore white coats and gas masks, even uglier and more frightening that those worn by the soldiers outside. These masks had bug-eyed lenses and they covered whole heads, seeming as if they *were* heads.

"I asked the other prisoners what was happening, and the only answer I received was from a girl a few years younger than me, who said, 'The men in the white coats want to make us demons.' I saw a soldier walk in and drag an old man out by the arm. He did not look as if he would survive the week, and he put up no resistance. The soldier placed the man into another chamber twenty feet away. It was similar to the one we were in, but smaller, with large tubes connected to its glass walls.

"One of the scientists yelled something in Chinese, and soon a gas that glowed a pale green color poured from the tubes. The old man just sat there pitifully, as the gas enveloped him. A heartbeat later I saw a scientist grin, pulling the corner of his collar to his lips and saying something I couldn't hear. The gas filtered out through ventilation shafts that were attached to the ceiling. There was a tense silence as the Chinese scientists and prisoners observed the old man.

"The old man flinched, then stood. We stared at what we thought was a hopeless victim shuffling toward the glass wall closest to the scientists' stations. I observed that the scientists didn't look the least bit surprised, as if they were used to this behavior. I jumped when I heard the beating and growling of what sounded like a beast of mythic proportions. The old man was pounding on the glass, his fists becoming bloodied with his attempts to break it. His muscles bulged noticeably larger between each strike and his growls grew louder by the second.

"After an hour of the horrific display, a scientist shouted something to a nearby soldier. The soldier saluted and went to the glass prison that held the demonic elder and slid open the door. The berserk man saw his chance for escape and charged the soldier. A muffled bang was heard. The old man spun in the air, blood trailing from his forehead. The soldier reloaded his pistol and walked off; a cleanup crew carried the body away on a stretcher.

"Another day passed before the scientists chose a new subject for their experiments. A scientist pointed at me, and my blood turned to ice. When the soldiers tried to take me into the glass room of horror, I resisted with all the strength I could muster. I was no match for the well fed and rested soldiers. Abruptly, a loud ringing sounded. They kicked me into the glass chamber and dashed off with the scientists trailing behind.

"What was happening? What is going on? Why were the prisoners left alone? Your soldiers had come to rescue us at that moment. I was put into a truck with the other test subjects and was shipped here."

Khurram's throat is dry from so much talking, and he drinks out of a water bottle that the older man in uniform offers him. The translation device is mechanically purring as it translates his last sentence. The interrogator nods and walks toward the door, the hinges making a horrible screeching noise as it opens and closes. From behind a one-way mirror, a young officer dressed in the battle fatigues of the Neo-NATO forces enters the room.

"What Mr. Khurram says matches the others' stories," says the young man, his accent revealing him as a native to Russia.

The older, balding man sighs and rubs his forehead with a sweaty hand, "I'm afraid so, Sergeant Debowska. Young man or not, we cannot take his testimony lightly."

"Yes sir. What should I tell the top brass?"

"Tell them, Sergeant, that our suspicions hold true. The Cathay are indeed creating a new biological weapon, and what is more troubling is that they care not who is its victim. If they manage to complete this weapon and use it against populated cities, God help us all."

A HERO WITH NO NAME
BY ARIAS JARRELLS

SILENCE. THAT'S ALL THAT surrounded me. It was always like that. I traveled through the shadows of the English streets like a ghost, and not one person took notice of me. My long, black hair touched no one as I passed the citizens; my silver-colored eyes only caught glimpses of myself in the windows of the shops. A goddess-like face looked back at me with matching eyes and an expression that showed indifference. Lips the color of a peach, skin kissed by a foreign sun, and the face shaped like a perfect heart. I wore a black trench coat zipped to protect the white shirt underneath, black jeans, high-heeled boots, and a cross belt containing three pouches. A sword was hanging from my hip. I saw this, but no other person did. They didn't care. They didn't know, and they never would. I had come to this country in search for my target, my rival, the one who had betrayed my family and my clan, causing their deaths. There was only two of my kind, the Dragaras, left: the murderer and me. Humans were her source of life, of power, and now she planned to kill them all in order to feed her horrid offspring. Yet people were not aware of this threat. They didn't see it or us.

It was raining as I walked directly into the streets. The only light was the moon and the streetlights. A perfect night. I proceeded into the dark corners of an alley and made my way to the roofs. I watched the people hurry to find shelter from the rain, but none would notice me watching them. I noted every detail and finally saw something of interest. A hooded figure was stocking a woman who was oblivious to the danger. Finally, something to do. I grinned and drew my sword from its sheath. It was a wide blade, long, strong, and sharp enough that even if it barely rested on my hand, it would cut. The blade itself was made out of black steel with silver swirls carved on it. The hilt of the weapon was like that of a rapier only larger due to the size of the blade.

I leapt off the roof and landed gracefully on the ground below. The figure could not see me nor could the woman. There was the sound of a rock being overturned, causing the woman to turn around. She screamed. The figure pounced then and placed its hand over her mouth. The woman tried again to scream but failed. My blood began to boil in both anger and excitement as I ran towards them. The figure saw me and screeched a loud high-pitched scream. The woman covered her ears, drops of crimson blood pouring from them. She would never be able to hear again. The figure pushed the woman aside and drew its own sword. The blade was arched and made of the strongest steel. I grinned. I knew who it was, or rather, what it was.

"Reveal yourself to me, Shadow Crawler!" I commanded.

The creature hissed, the hood flew backwards to reveal the face of a Shadow Crawler. Its face resembled that of a vulture with its scalp covered with a black shell, like that of a scarab. It was a creature born from my rival, Nis'tai. The monster snarled then burst into a puff of black smoke. I stood on guard, looking around to be sure that it didn't catch my back. I placed my sword back in its sheath while fumbling through one of my pouches for a vial. I heard its screech again. I looked up and saw the Shadow Crawler leap across the roofs away from me. I followed on foot, running with the speed that no mortal being could match. Yet running was only half the fun. I climbed up the fire escape of an apartment and then raced across the roofs with the beast. It leapt away and then made a sharp turn to the left, toward an abandoned church. My home. I growled while leaping into the air, soaring for a moment before giant black wings sprouted from my back. I took flight, flying even faster than I could run. I looked to the church and saw a multitude of pesky Shadow Crawlers perched on top. Anger stirred within me. I landed on the tip of a tower and glared at the monsters as they too looked at me with their pupil-less eyes.

They screeched before stepping aside for their mistress and mother. A woman no older than twenty stepped forward with sword in hand. My target had now appeared. She sneered down at me, revealing her fangs.

"Hello there, my sweet Yoko. How good of you to stop by," she cooed in a slimy voice.

I snorted. "Nis'tai, sending your henchmen to do your dirty work? What a coward."

She laughed, her voice sounding like high-pitched wind chimes.

"Of course, Yoko. How else am I to get your attention? I see that you were able to save the woman, but not her hearing."

"What do you want?"

"You know what I want. I want all mankind to suffer as we have. They do not see us; let us give them something to see. Let them see their own blood!"

"Not while I still breathe air."

"Well then…" She burst into a plume of smoke and reappeared in front of me. "…we have a problem."

She swung her blade at me, but I saw it in time to duck. I took a step back and growled. Drawing my sword, I took a fighting stance. She only giggled in a mocking tone before she lunged at me again. We crossed blades. Sparks flew in every direction as we exchanged blows. She thrust her sword forward, missing me only by a few inches. I grabbed it with my free hand and punched her in the face. She stumbled back, regaining her balance on the rail of the roof. I quickly pulled out a vial and popped the lid open.

"Hey Nis'tai, say ahhhh!" She turned her head as I splashed the contents of the vial in her face.

She shrieked and covered her face as steam emitted from her skin. "You little brat!" she screamed.

I grinned, twirling the empty vial in my fingers. She took her hands away from her face. It was swollen with boils covering her flesh. Her face was melting off to reveal her true face, the face of a dragon queen, ugly and horrifying. The Shadow Crawlers hissed and screeched at the sight of their wounded mistress. Nis'tai roared and tackled me, causing us to fall off the roof. I stretched my wings and caught the soft breeze that blew my way. She sprouted a pair of dragon wings and came at me again. I dodged another blow. She tried to strike again, but she was so blinded by rage and the heavy downpour of rain that she couldn't tell where I was. I had the advantage here. I didn't have to see her. All I had to do was listen for her heartbeat. I sheathed my sword and flew around her, causing her to panic.

"This ends now, Nis'tai. You've terrorized this world for too long. You killed my family, murdered the innocent, and stole the souls of countless people. Your judgment day has come."

Her breathing quickened. Her heartbeat sounded like a drum, every beat growing louder and quicker. I drew a small dagger from the side of my belt and prepared myself to give the final blow. I drew closer and closer with every moment, yet I was stopped when she swung her blade in my direction.

"You little beast. You think that you can defeat me? I'll just come back and kill you. You're weak. You don't have the guts to kill your own kind."

I gripped the dagger tighter, "That's what you think, Nis'tai."

I flew in for the final blow, but before I could deliver it, one of the Shadow Crawlers cried out to her, "Mistress! Behind you!"

She whirled around and drove her sword forward. She struck me in the side, cutting into my flesh. I yelped out and drew back as she swung again. I felt the warmth of my blood trickling off my fingertips. I had to be quick now. The more blood I lost, the less focused I became. I dodged another blow and then created some distance between us. Leaving her to swing at the open air again, I placed my dagger back in my belt and drew my sword. I took a deep, shuddering breath and raised the blade up into the air, chanting,

"Sword of darkness,
Sword of might,
Blade that was made to slay the Mistress of the Wicked,
Return to your true form,
To end this evil once and for all."

I felt power course through my veins. My sword began to glow a golden color as it transformed. When the glowing ceased, there in my hands was a scythe with the same blade pattern as the sword it was before. Nis'tai drew closer. She swung her blade again, catching my shoulder with its cold edge. It cut into the skin, but not as deep as the wound in my side. I hissed, pain surging through me.

This was the end for both of us. I brought the blade of the scythe down and the sound of tearing flesh and broken bones rang through the night. I heard a scream, then a thud as Nis'tai's body hit the ground far below. The Shadow Crawlers cried out before they vanished from the earth. My deed was done. I had no more purpose in this world.

I slowly flew back to the roof of the church and landed clumsily. I rolled onto the flat surface and lay there in silence. The scythe returned to the blade it once was while my wings disappeared in a plume of feathers. My blood mixed with the rain and dripped off the edge, onto the gargoyles below. My hair was matted to my forehead, my breathing become shallow and harder to control. My time had come.

Come morning no one would know what had happened. They wouldn't know my name or what I had done for them. Humans were like that. They never knew me or my face. They would never know I sacrificed my life for theirs. As long as their lives were undisturbed, they didn't care. I closed my eyes as I felt my life slip away. I was the hero with no name.

LISTEN
BY PRISCILLA PORTILLO

"I'M NOT GOING TO. I don't want to hurt him," she says.

"You're just hurting him more by not doing the right thing. It's for the best for both of you. Listen, the longer you are together, the deeper he is going to fall for you, and you'll just have pity for him," I tell her. I try to reason with her, but it doesn't seem to work.

"I told you already. I don't want to break his heart. I don't want to see his face drown in tears right in front of me," she retorts angrily and tosses her black hair behind her in a huff. She looks at me with her dark eyes, tempting me to challenge her.

"Well, maybe if you wait longer you will get to see him drown in tears and then go do something stupid. Do you prefer that?" I yell at her. I wait for her answer. She just stares at the ground.

"I'll make sure he doesn't do that," she says weakly.

"What? You think it's as simple as that? You know he's crazy about you, Marisol. You shouldn't be playing with him like this."

"You know what? You're just making my head spin, so if you aren't going to help then I think it's best you leave," she orders.

"Marisol, we're best friends. You said you needed my help, so I'm trying to help you. The point of my advice is for you to just listen. It's supposed to help you decide. But I guess you don't want it anymore, so I'll just leave. You can do whatever the hell you want." I get my things and leave her sitting alone at our table in the school cafeteria. I throw away my lunch at a nearby trash can, except for my orange juice.

As I'm drinking my juice, I think about all the times Marisol has done this to me. She never really seems to pay attention to my thoughts and opinions. All the arguments we've had have been mostly related to the guys we liked.

We always end up constantly debating on "why he's the right one." I'm right most of the time though, I think defiantly. Jason is a sweet but reckless guy, a year older than us, who graduated from high school last year. We're all friends and had a lot of fun hanging out together, until he got a crush on Marisol.

As for this argument, I'm definitely sure I'm right. How could she continue being with Jason without having much feeling for him? The only reason why she got with him was so that her ex would know she was taken and leave her alone. Plus, she knew Jason had a thing for her, so it seemed to her a perfect plan. But poor Jason! He really likes her. I think he even has an obsession with her. I just hope he doesn't get hurt badly if Marisol actually listens to me.

"Ring!" The loud noise of the bell interrupts my thoughts. Hesitatingly, I go to class, knowing I'll have to see Marisol there. To my chagrin, she is standing there by the classroom door. I pull my caramel-colored hair back, getting ready for another argument that awaits me. Although she is a few inches taller than me, she's never been able to intimidate me.

"Hey Amber, I thought about what you told me during lunch," she says in a tiny, contrite voice. "And I figured you are right. I'm going to stand up to Jason today or tomorrow and break up with him, whether he likes it or not."

Her sudden change of mind catches me by surprise.

"And I'm sorry for yelling at you," she continues. "Will you forgive me?"

"Uh…" I stumble for an answer. "Uh, well, since you finally agree with me, sure." I laugh and she joins in.

Melodic sounds wake me up in the middle of the night. It's my cell phone ringing. I sit up and grab it. My eyes hurt with the bright light facing me. It's Marisol. Half-awake, I answer the phone. "Hello?"

"Amber, Amber, I'm scared! Will you please help me?"

Her panicked voice alerts me, and I sit up straighter. "What's the matter?" I ask, with an obviously concerned tone.

"I went through with it," she answers. "I dumped Jason. I tried to explain that I don't have feelings for him and that our relationship is pretty much pointless in the nicest possible way. I tried to make it seem like it wasn't such a big deal, but he got out of hand."

"Oh my God, Marisol, what did he do?" I was already thinking the worst because with Jason, you could never know what might happen.

"Well, he started to cry, and I did too because I felt sad for him. He made me feel really bad because he said that I just played with his heart," she says, her voice shaky.

"I thought he might do something crazy."

"Well, that's what I'm afraid of. Afterwards, he was leaving and then he stopped, turned back, and shouted that he couldn't believe I had done this to him and that he really loved me, and that he would even kill himself for me. Then he cursed at me and left running," she says, her voice jagged with crying. "You really gotta help me. I'm nervous and scared."

I think for a while, then say, "Well, since we don't have an idea of where Jason could be, how about if we drop by his apartment to make sure he's okay?"

"Amber, that is an excellent idea," she exclaims.

"Thanks, but where do we meet?"

"At the liquor store. I'll pick you up in five minutes." She hangs up the phone.

I get up and check the time. It's three in the morning. Yawning, I get dressed. I sneak out of my house and go wait for Marisol around the corner. It's still dark. I look up and see the full moon lit brightly on the eastern sky. Then I look down the street and see Marisol's parents' car approaching me. I wave my hands so she can see me. She stops the car, and I jump in.

"Thanks for helping me, Amber."

"Oh it's okay," I respond. "That's what best friends are for."

We drive toward Jason's apartment. It's a rundown complex where he can afford the rent. Despite the deserted streets, it seems to take forever to get there.

We're quiet until Marisol blurts out in a whisper, "I'm so scared."

"I'm sure it's going to be okay," I mutter softly. "But if he doesn't answer his door, how are we going to get in?"

"I know where he keeps a spare key."

"Good."

We try the elevator, but as usual, it's out of order. We have to run up ten flights of stairs. We're gasping, our hearts pounding.

"If only the elevator worked," says Marisol. "The suspense is killing me."

"If only Jason didn't live on the eleventh floor."

"I know, huh?" Marisol bends down to get the key from underneath the flower pot on the window sill by his door. She shows me the silver copy. "Told ya," she says. She opens the door and we step in. The lights are all on. There's broken glass from who-knows-where and empty beer cans lying everywhere. Lots of stuff has been knocked off the table and shelves and shattered on the floor.

My eyes skim the mess and look toward the sliding glass door leading to the balcony. It's open. "Oh no," I exclaim. I run outside and look over the balcony railing expecting the worst, but there is no one down below. I sigh with relief. I go back in and slide the door shut.

"What?" asks Marisol.

"He's not there, like lying down there on the ground."

"Oh! You got me scared." Then her eyes widen. "Do you here that?"

"Hear what? Water running?"

"Yeah, it's coming from the bathroom. Let's go check it out."

We head toward the bathroom. Marisol opens the door and freezes in place. I peer around her. The tub is overflowing with water and Jason is halfway in, head first. Marisol's face is pale and her eyes are wide and watery. She stares in shock.

I react. I try to pull Jason out of the tub, but he's too heavy. "Marisol, come on! Help me."

She snaps out of it, and together we're able to drag him onto the floor. His face is pale and he doesn't seem to be breathing. I shut off the faucet, asking, "Do you know CPR?"

"No," she says between hysterical cries.

"Neither do I. Stay with him." I run out of the apartment, screaming, "Help! Help!" I bang on the neighbors' doors and one of them opens.

A man sticks his head out. "What's the matter? Why are you screaming?"

I shudder and point at Jason's apartment door, yelling, "We need an ambulance!"

"What's wrong with Jason?" He dashes inside the apartment, finds Jason, and starts CPR on him, while I get my phone out of my purse and dial 911.

It seems like hours before the ambulance arrives, when actually it's only minutes. The paramedics take Jason away on a stretcher, and Marisol and the neighbor decide to ride with him in the ambulance. I hear Marisol call my name from within the vehicle. I look inside. Jason is strapped onto a respirator, but not yet breathing on his own, and Marisol is seated beside him.

She glares back at me. "You know what I learned from this, Amber? That I shouldn't listen to everything you say," she yells and shuts the door in my face.

SHADOW MEN
BY ALEXANDRIA TERAN

*D*ON'T STOP RUNNING*! KEEP running! Don't look back!*
My heart pounds in rhythm with the echo of my footsteps as I run through the alley. Other footsteps fall right behind me, moving closer.

"Stop!" a man's voice bounces against the close brick walls.

Click. Behind me a hand gun is cocked. I feel the sweat drip from my face as my legs pump harder. *Bang!* A bullet flies by my head.

Will everything I've done, everything I've been through go down the drain because of these two Shadow Men, whom I know I can take? I think not!

My speed picks up. There's an opening in the alley way. I run to the right, stop, press against the wall, waiting for my enemies. Pulling out my dagger, I count one, two three. Their footsteps draw near. Four, five, six. The first one comes into view. Caught by surprise, he raises his gun. I swing my dagger at his face. *Hit!* Again. *Hit!* Again. *Hit!*

"Three strikes and you're out," I mutter, kicking his side as he lies dead on the ground.

A sharp sting comes across my face reminding me there are still more Shadow Men to battle. As I resume fighting, my loved one's voice plays in my head. *"That's it, Julia. Don't stop. Keep attacking."*

I've never fought. Well, I've never been in danger until that afternoon when my daughter, Alessandra and I were playing outside in the front yard of our small cabin, surrounded by woods. The green grass is trimmed on the inside of our fence and tall on the outside. The wind blew gently, slowly bringing the dark clouds in.

"Ales, I'll be right back. Mommy has to hang the sheets."

"Okay, Mommy."

I walked to the back of the cabin. I never realized what could happen in only a minute.

"Mommy!" Ales' scream soared out of the woods. I ran toward it.

"Ales!" My voice began to choke as I ran through the woods. No sign of my daughter anywhere.

"Mommy! Mommy!"

"Alessandra?!" I ran deeper into the woods, and still couldn't find her.

"Mommy!" She sat on the ground holding her knee, blood dripping through her fingers.

"What are you doing here? What did I tell you about the woods?"

"To stay away from them."

I've always made sure to play it safe, to stay away from danger, to run and hide, not stay and fight. After Alessandra was born, I became even more afraid of everything, for her sake.

"Come on, Ales. We'll go home and take care of your knee." I lifted her into my arms. Her soft, brown eyes began to turn dark brown like her father's under the darkness of the clouds. Her long, black hair, like mine, was a silk blanket draped over my arms. Her round cheeks and dimpled smile always brought a warm, comfortable feeling to me. She was mine, my perfect little angel, whom I would go to the ends of the world to protect.

"Julia! What happened?" My husband Israel's voice was filled with concern and anger as he saw the blood on Ales' knee.

"She's fine. She scraped her knee is all."

Later than night, when I walked into the living room, Israel asked, "Where's Ales?"

"In bed." I looked at him, his soft, light brown skin glowing in the firelight. His dark eyes looked black from a distance, but when I came nearer, they teased me with a hint of brown. As he smiled his cheeks rounded, making his face a perfect circle.

"What?" he smirked.

"Nothing. I was just thinking Ales looks a lot like you, more than me. And that's not right. She's a girl, so she should look like her mother." His laugh made me smile.

He grabbed my hand and pulled me onto his lap. "I love you," he whispered into my ear.

I placed a kiss on his cheek. "I love you, too."

"Okay, time for bed." Israel wrapped his arms around me and set me on my feet. Laughing, we climbed the stairs. As we passed Ales' room, her little voice spilled from the crack of the door.

"Mommy said I had to stay out of the woods. I got hurt last time."

"Ales?" My heart froze when I opened the door. At the edge of her bed, a tall shadow leaned over her. Before Israel could tackle whatever it was, the figure was gone, leaving nothing but coldness hovering in Ales' room.

"Ales! Who was that? Who were you talking to?"

"My friend, Mommy. I was playing with him in the woods today."

We brought her into our room to sleep. I didn't sleep at all. I was afraid that thing would come back. Who was he? What did he want? How the hell did he get into my child's room?

I went downstairs to get a drink of water. I took a sip. *Crash!* The glass fell from my hand and shattered on the tile floor. A face stared at me through the window, smiling, flashing yellow teeth that stuck out from a pale face. His pupils were pitch black, covering most of his eyes. Instantly, he was gone.

I ran upstairs, taking two steps at a time, knowing that thing would be in our room after my daughter.

"Israel!" My scream filled the cabin. Clutching a dagger, the thing hovered over my husband. Israel awoke and grabbed his shotgun. *Bang!* Ales awoke screaming.

"Run, Julia! Take Ales!

I grabbed Ales and I ran downstairs and out the door toward the jeep. I fumbled with the keys and tried to start the car, yelling at Ales to get in her car seat. Israel came running out of the cabin, firing one last time before jumping into the car. I shifted the car into reverse, and then to first. I stomped on the gas pedal and drove as fast as the jeep would go.

"Where do we go, Israel?"

"The other side of the woods. We need to go to my family."

"Israel, no! We made a pact."

"Julia, you know who that was. They're going to keep coming, and you know that. We need to go somewhere safe, and you know the only safe place is with my family."

Israel was no ordinary man. I didn't know that until after we married, nine years ago. I knew nothing of his family, so he decided to show me why he kept his family a secret. Israel and his family are a breed of super humans. They don't age like normal people; Israel is actually seventy-six, not twenty-eight. They're strong, heal fast, and never get sick. They don't know why they are the way they are. They live deep in the woods far from civilization. Centuries ago humans discovered their race, known as the Ouranos, and saw them as monsters and the devil's work. Humans believed they killed off the last of the Ouranos, but the humans were wrong. The remaining Ouranos don't take the chance of being discovered, so they hide deep in the woods.

They build their own homes and only go into the city when their supplies are low. They all live together and never leave for the fear of their safety. Israel was the first to leave, for my sake, and his family never liked me. That's why I don't want to go back, that and because of Ales. Israel and I made a pact not to ever tell her about his family. When there are those who are stronger, there are others who wants them dead. Those who want the Ouranos dead are the Shadow Men.

The Shadow Men were once humans, until they came across Ouranos. They envied the Ouranos, believing that once they captured them, the Shadow Men could figure out how to become a super race like them and control all mankind. The Shadow Men soon found out that they could not catch the Ouranos, so they turned to dark magic and sold themselves to the devil in exchange for super powers. Soon they found out that the devil tricked them and doomed them to an eternal curse of profound ugliness. The Shadow Men swore their vengeance on the Ouranos and vowed to kill them all.

The woods where Israel's family lives has an open clearing. Tall, green trees surround and protect them from intruders and curious eyes. Each home is lined up, in a different color and design.

When we were within twenty yards of the entrance of the property, ten armed warriors leaped in front of our jeep. One by one they pulled their matching semi- automatic hand guns from their holsters and aimed them at me. They all knew who we were, and none wanted me around.

The grandson of the very first Ourano, now one of the eldest of the family, stood at the door of his home. A look of disgust made his old face look like death. "What are you doing here? You know you two are not welcome here."

"The Shadow Men attacked me and my daughter, Erick," explained Israel. "I'm sure they'll attack again." Israel stood tall and wrapped an arm around Ales, his half-Ourano, half-human daughter, showing he did not care whether he was welcomed or not.

"Come," said Erick. "We'll talk in private. Your wife and child can stay in the unoccupied house next door."

Erick and Israel talked for hours. I put Ales to sleep and I paced through the house, fearing the Shadow Man would return. Finally, Israel walked through the front door with anger killing his face.

"What did Erick say?"

"He isn't going to help. He wants us to leave. Apparently we're putting the family in danger, even though he's got a whole army of warriors to fight for us."

I hugged him. "Israel, we can take care of ourselves. Let Ales sleep while we go outside, so you can teach me to fight, and in the morning we'll leave."

We asked one of Erick's maids to watch Ales while we trained. Erick was generous enough to open his armory to us. His collection was unique with weapons from the Middle Ages as well as modern times. We chose a selection of guns, blades, and daggers, and began training in the moonlight.

"That's it, Julia. Don't stop. Keep attacking."

We trained for hours, until the sun came up. But as the sun's rays shone through the trees, they revealed black figures in the distance. The Shadow Men charged toward us so fast, they seemed to fly.

"Run, Julia, run!"

We ran toward the homes, screaming to warn those unprepared. All the children and women ran to the basement of their homes. The Shadow Men were getting closer, and as the armed warriors charged toward them. I followed, ready to fight.

"Julia, no. Go protect Ales." Israel kissed me and ran toward the Shadow Men.

Three of the five Shadow Men attacked the Ourano men; the other two ran into the house where Ales and some others hid. Four of the warriors and I ran after them. Pulling out my nine millimeter hand gun, I shot one Shadow Man in the shoulder. Of course that made him mad, and he turned to attack me with his sword. I shot two rounds at his chest and one at the side of his neck. He fell to the ground, and before he could get up, I stabbed my blade into his throat. As I stood looking down at the Shadow Man's motionless body I knew all fear I had was gone.

The four Ourano warriors who were helping me had been killed. The second Shadow Man grinned at me, his yellow fangs sending chills down my spine. He looked toward the house that Ales was hiding in and continued running toward it. I ran as fast as I could, reloading my gun. A women's scream came from the house and then a child's cry. I ran into the basement to find the Shadow Man holding my daughter.

"Mommy!" Tears slid down Ales' face.

"Leave her alone!" I screamed.

He placed his arm around Ales' chest and the other hand on her chin. Before I could shoot him, he twisted her head and held her body. A crack echoed through the basement. My daughter's small, lifeless body fell to the floor with a soft thud. I screamed and shot nine rounds while moving toward the thing. Four shots to the chest, two to its leg, and three to its face. As it fell to the floor, I pulled out my blade and stabbed it in the neck and chest over and over.

"Julia?"

I turned to the door were Israel stood. I was crying and covered in the Shadow Man's blood. I looked down at Ales' body, her once warm, smiling face had turned pale and her lips blue. I fell to my knees pulling her body close to me. I heard Israel begin to cry. When I looked up at him, I saw a Shadow Man sneaking up behind him. Before Israel could pull his gun, the Shadow Man's sword stabbed into his chest, piercing his heart.

I held Ales closer and closed my eyes, not caring to live anymore. I heard the Shadow Man's footsteps slowly approaching, knowing I would soon be with my husband and daughter in death. Nine shots were fired, and I heard a loud thud. When I looked up, Erick was in the door way and the lifeless Shadow Man's body was on the floor.

Remembering that night, I walk away from the two lifeless Shadow Men I have just killed in the alley. That night, I lost everything I needed to live. My daughter was my life, and my husband my soul. Now that I walk this world alone, I am soulless, I am lifeless. Nothing can take me from this world until I have killed every last Shadow Men who has killed me.

MUD AND BLOOD
BY T. W. ADAMS

WILHELM WOKE TO THE boom of a nearby artillery shell. "Dammit," he muttered, opening his eyes. Sleep was hard to come by in the trenches, and the barracks were little comfort from the wasteland outside. He glanced down at his grumbling stomach, and wished that the British would surrender so he could go home. Looking up, he noticed a new letter placed on top of his pack, and could guess who it was from. What would his mother think of him? He remembered her worried face, and his father's proud smile as his boy went off to serve the Fatherland. He had to admit, he was excited when he boarded that train. But things were so different now. So different.

Wilhelm sat up and reached for the letter addressed *Gefreiter* Wilhelm Dirkschneider, Fourth *Heer Infanterie Korps*. He opened the envelope, and unfolding the paper, saw his mother's familiar handwriting.

> 19 *Juli* 1917
>
> Dearest Wilhelm,
>
> We all miss you very much. Your *vater* is so proud of you. I worry about you every day. Is it really as bad as they say it is on the front? I hope you are eating well. I'm sure the British will surrender soon. That is what the Kaiser says, at least. I hope he is right. When you get back you must tell us all your stories. Till is growing fast. He always talks about how he wants to be just like his big *bruder*. I don't know if you will get this letter by your birthday, but when you get back we will have a proper celebration for you. Even at nineteen you are still *meine* little boy. I hope

you are having a little bit of fun seeing the world. When you come back you can tell us how Belgium is. *Ich liebe dich.*

With *Liebe,*

Your *Mutter*

How was Belgium? Cold and wet. Regardless of the fact that it was the middle of summer. Wilhelm stood up, leaving the letter on his bunk. Putting his *stahlhelm* on his head, and grabbing his Mauser rifle, he walked outside to the *graben.* The sun was just beginning to rise, but no birds chirped. Wilhelm continued down the trench, nodding to nervous men as he passed them. He wasn't overly worried about an attack from the British today. It had rained especially hard last night and sending men over the wall now would make for a slow approach in the mud. With the amount of *maschinengewehr* nests dotting the German lines, any assault would be suicide, and it was far too wet for tanks. Wilhelm continued forward, seeing a familiar soldier, who leaned against the trench wall.

"Ah *hallo, meine freund*!" the man greeted him.

"*Guten Morgen,* Erich!" Wilhelm replied, smiling and grasping his friend's hand. "Shouldn't you be at your gun?" .

Erich was a man of average height, with a stocky build. He had dirty blond hair, and always seemed to have a five o'clock shadow on his face. Erich was a machine gunner who tore men to pieces with his MG 08. Wilhelm was always impressed by his gentle face. "It's like a swamp out here. I doubt we'll see any action. But I understand it's your birthday today. How old are you?"

"*Neunzehn.*"

"Ah, nineteen! Barely shaving, but old enough to kill a man, eh?"

"I feel closer to ninety."

"I know what you mean. To hell with this war."

They ducked as an artillery shell whistled over their heads and exploded somewhere beyond their trench.

"*Scheiße*" Erich said, grimacing. "I'd hate to go that way. At least in no man's land you can face your enemy. *Zigarette?* My treat. It's your birthday."

"*Ja, danke.*" Wilhelm took the cigarette and the matches that Erich offered him. Nothing calmed his nerves better. "I don't know what will kill me. A bullet or boredom."

Erich chuckled. "There are a lot of ways to die, my friend. Who knows? Maybe you'll get lucky and drown in the mud."

"Well, I would definitely prefer that to choking on poison gas."

Wilhelm noticed one of the fresher recruits looking at them with wide eyes. That was himself, not too long ago. Erich was twenty-three, twenty-four maybe. Practically an old man compared to most of the soldiers in the trenches. He had survived the war long enough to remember wearing a *picklehaube*. Wilhelm had liked how they looked and was disappointed that he wasn't issued one, but he changed his opinion when Erich told him he had dozed off wearing his, leaning against a trench wall, and a British soldier had shot the spike clean off. The *picklehaube* gave away troop positions, while the *stahlhelm* provided better protection from shrapnel.

Another shell whistled nearby and landed close to them. Wilhelm could see dirt fly farther down the trench and was glad he had stopped to chat with Erich. Before either could speak, a soldier named Joseph came sprinting in their direction, yelling *"Angriff! Angriff! Die British sind angreifen! Angriff!"*

His words faded as other shouts erupted throughout the trenches.

Erich gripped Wilhelm's shoulders, and with a smile, exclaimed, "Happy Birthday!" before climbing into his machine gun nest.

Are the British insane, attacking in these conditions?

Wilhelm peered over the trench wall to see Entente troops charging forward. Looking down the sights of his Mauser, he picked out his target, an enemy soldier drawing a grenade. He waited for him to pull the pin, then fired and hit his shoulder. As the man stumbled, the grenade fell and exploded in a shower of mud and blood.

One.

Wilhelm pulled back the bolt on his rifle, letting the empty bullet casing fall to the ground, then loaded a new bullet into the chamber and pushed the bolt forward.

Many of the advancing soldiers were cut down by machine-gun fire, their bodies hurdled by the soon-dead men behind them. Eventually, the men began crouching down in artillery craters. Aiming at a man sprinting for one of the craters, Wilhelm squeezed off another shot. His prey lost his footing an instant before the bullet could penetrate his chest and was spared. The man behind him was not so lucky.

Wilhelm saw his accidental victim fall to his knees, blood spurting from his neck and mouth. Cocking his gun, Wilhelm lined up another shot, which struck the dying man in the forehead.

Two.

Wilhelm continued unleashing death upon the Entente Forces, pausing only to reload every five rounds. Many enemy soldiers died, but more surged forward. They were approaching closer.

The closest attackers began to crawl, cutting their way through the barb wire protecting the first line of German trenches. In one swift motion,

Wilhelm removed a *granate* from his satchel, pulled the pin, and threw it. It landed near a very young soldier, struggling with his wire cutters. The boy scrambled to get away, tearing his face and arms on the snarl of sharp metal surrounding him.

Seeing the boy's predicament, another Brit who looked shockingly like him, dove onto the grenade. The man closed his eyes tight, waiting for death.

Nothing happened.

Looking at the boy for whom he had nearly sacrificed his life, he yelled, "Simon! It's okay. It's a du–" and was cut off by the delayed detonation of Wilhelm's grenade.

Wilhelm aimed at the boy, now frozen in terror and anguish. Bringing the sight to his eye, Wilhelm readied himself for another kill. Before he could pull the trigger, he heard a *bang* to his left and saw the boy crumple. Turning toward the shot, Wilhelm saw Erich with his Luger pistol still aimed at the corpse. "Wilhelm, we're being overrun! We need to fall back to the second line!"

Fritz von Lossberg, *Oberst* in the Imperial German Army, was a defensive expert who set up the four lines of defense that the Fourth Army occupied outside of the town of Ypres. The first line had just failed.

Cries in both English and German filled the air. Some of the British had made it through the barb wire, and were entering the German trench. It had been a while since Wilhelm needed to use his bayonet, and he didn't want to change that.

"C'mon, Wilhelm! An Iron Cross doesn't matter when you're dead!"

Following Erich through the chaos, Wilhelm witnessed other Germans retreating as well. Finding a ramp out of the trench, they escaped to the surface. The next line of defense was about a hundred-fifty meters behind them. If they could put enough distance between themselves and any following British, they could make a stand at the next trench and prevent more ground from being taken. Turning to look behind him, Wilhelm saw that many of the British soldiers were confused, and didn't know if they should follow. Their indecision provided the Germans with valuable time.

Retreating through the mud, Erich and Wilhelm heard bullets cutting through the air around them. The second line was now just thirty meters away. The soldiers in the second trench, realizing the first line had been taken, gave cover fire to the retreating soldiers. Wilhelm heard a whiz and a soft thud.

Erich cried out and fell to the ground, clutching his leg. Rushing to aid him, Wilhelm was stunned to see Erich laughing.

"So damn close! So damn close! And a Brit shoots me in the damn leg!"

Wilhelm wrapped Erich's arm around his shoulders and supported him as he hopped on one leg.

"Don't be so sad. Maybe you'll get to go home!" said Wilhelm. "C'mon. We're almost there!"

Many of the Germans lucky enough to escape were now leaping into the second trench. When the machine guns opened fire on the following British, it was their turn to retreat. As Wilhelm and Erich approached the trench, several men helped them down. Wilhelm gently set Erich on the driest spot he could find. His leg was bleeding. Badly.

"*Sanitäter!*" yelled Wilhelm. "Medic!"

"Will-Wilhelm..." Erich's voice grew weaker.

"The medic's coming! It's just a shot to the leg!"

"Take my Luger..." Erich extended his shaky hand, barely holding onto his pistol.

Wilhelm took the gun from his dying friend.

"Another birthday present." Erich smiled, then closed his eyes. All expression faded from his face.

Too late, a man carrying bandages rushed up to examine Erich's leg. "The bullet penetrated the main artery," he told Wilhelm. "I'm sorry." The *sanitäter* departed in search of other wounded men. Wilhelm was left alone.

Now he had a story for his family. He could tell them how his friend had bled to death on his birthday.

ONE NIGHT
BY HILARY ALEXANDRIA SPIVEY

*G*REAT! HOLLY GRAHAM THOUGHT as she felt herself lose her balance on a mound of dirt. Everything was in chaos around her, and she was following this stranger she met by the keg. *Met by the keg! What was I thinking?* she said to herself as she fled the last warehouse party of the year.

The warehouse was where all the students from the local high school got together and threw parties. She had never been to a warehouse party, and had heard that they got out of control sometimes. She hadn't worried about this during all the loud music, dancing, and drinking, not until the cops started chasing them out. The chopper lights beamed in through the ceiling windows and sirens blared. Right before she lost her balance, she was running in the parking lot, not knowing where she was going, following a guy whose name she didn't even know. Now she was falling and thinking for sure she would get caught by the police because she didn't have a ride, and then she would lose her scholarship and wouldn't be able to go to college and... A warm hand tugged on her elbow, helping her recover from her stumble before she hit the ground.

"Come on, hurry! We gotta get outta here!" the stranger said, pulling her toward the back row of cars. In the spotlight of the helicopter, she recognized him from her school's baseball team. Relief trickled through her as she thought, *He can't be a mass murderer; I would have heard about it in this small town.* They reached a beat up Chevy pickup she assumed was his, because he gave her a boost in, then got in himself and drove off.

Chad Brigson thought, *How do I get myself into these things?* as he turned his truck onto a back road to head back into town. He glanced over at the girl sitting in the passenger seat. She looked familiar, probably from his school. He searched her face, looking for an invitation to start a conversation. She caught his eye, and her lips turned up at the corners, almost producing a smile. *Wow. It lights up her whole face*, he thought, as he shifted his attention to the road.

"So, does this sorta thing always happen at these parties?" she asked, a nervous shake creeping into her voice.

"Um no, not usually. Most times the cops surround the place first and fire a few shots." Chad watched the horror sink into her face. She was pretty, average, but pretty, with black, curly hair and deep blue eyes. At the party he had thought, *I have to find out who this chick is!* He hadn't had time to even ask her her name before they had to bolt. He saw the town marquee up ahead, flashing an Iowa Mid-state Fair advertisement, and decided to pull over and get to know her. He parked under one of the few street lights in the small country town.

"So, hi. I'm Chad."

Holly had never been in a situation like this before, and had never been the type of girl who was outgoing or outspoken around strangers. She tended to be quiet and kept to herself. "Oh, hi. I'm Holly Graham," she said robotically, sticking her hand out for him to shake and feeling a hot blush creep into her cheeks.

"Well, Holly Graham," he said with a chuckle, shaking her hand. "What do you suppose we do now?"

Holly wasn't sure if there was an underlying meaning to his question, but she decided his eyes looked sincere, with amusement spreading over his features. Beneath the street light, she was able to really see him for the first time. He had dark brown hair with green eyes and a light bend in his nose like it had been broken. He was wearing a navy blue letterman jacket that had a baseball on it. "Well, it's almost eleven o'clock, so I guess you could just take me home," she said, hoping he would. Although she was intrigued by him, their situation was unsettling.

"Yeah," Chad said, pondering the thought, then adding, "Or I know something better." She looked surprised, but didn't reply. Part of him was telling himself to take her home and go meet up with his buddies, but a bigger part was telling him to find out more about her. *Get a grip Chad. She probably just wants to go home and talk to her boyfriend or something.*

He sped down Main Street, not knowing where they were going. They passed the drugstore and the shoe store. The town of 15,000 looked completely shut down, even though it was fairly early on a Saturday night. A small light beamed from the ice cream store. He slammed on his brakes, stopping in the middle of the road.

"Ice cream?"

"Not if I have to die for it!" Holly yelled at him, her heart racing, as she braced herself against the dashboard.

"Oh come on, I wasn't going that fast, and there's no one around." He was glad he had gotten a rise out of her. She had been too nervous and shy, and he wanted to see the real her, under all that reserve. They pulled up to the ice cream store only to find it closed.

"Great, we almost died for nothing," she said, rolling her eyes.

"Not quite," he answered, spotting an ice cream vending machine across the street. He left her in his truck and went to get two ice cream sandwiches. When he returned, he pulled down the tailgate and sat. "It's gonna melt if you don't come and get it," he called back to the cab of the truck.

Holly got out and joined him, taking the ice cream sandwich and settling next to him on the tailgate.

"So what were you doing at the party anyway?" Chad asked.

"To be honest, I'm not even sure. I thought it would be fun. I've heard so much about them, and how glorious they would be, so I decided to go," she answered, not knowing why she told him her whole story. Before he could comment, she added, "You're a senior right?"

"Yeah, and more then ready to graduate."

"Yeah, me too."

"So tell me about yourself, Holly Graham."

"Well, there's not much to tell. Just a senior, got into a college on the West Coast. I'm an only child. I own a dog and two cats." She looked at the ground. "Yup, that about sums me up." She didn't know why, but she felt comfortable with Chad. Instinctively, she trusted him. "What about you?"

"Same with me––not much to tell. Senior, got a full ride baseball scholarship. Got two older sisters, no animals, and I don't like Cheetos."

"You don't like Cheetos? That's absurd. I don't think I've ever known anyone who doesn't like Cheetos," said Holly, laughing so hard she almost began to choke.

Chad scooted closer to her and slapped her back, thinking that things were going better than he expected. She was even funny when she let her guard down. She had a beautiful smile, and he wanted to make her laugh more.

For the next few hours they sat talking like old friends. Chad hung onto to every word that she said in telling stories of when she was a little girl. He was interested why her family moved from Chicago to this small town. He listened to her dreams of moving back to the big city and becoming a doctor. He felt she had the brains and the talent, and just needed confidence in herself.

Holly was amazed that Chad didn't know what he wanted to do with his life. She had never had that problem and wanted to understand his indecision. She had never been confused about anything in life. What to wear some days, she had no clue, but when it came to what she would be doing in five years, she had a plan, made and memorized. They both sat there talking, trying to understand each other in an attempt to understand themselves.

As Holly was telling Chad about her first loose tooth, the town clock chimed four.

"Oh my God! Four o'clock! I'm gonna be dead!" Holly said franticly as she scooted off the tailgate.

"What, do you have a curfew?"

"Yeah, it's midnight. Would you take me home now?" she asked, already heading toward the cab. She had never come in past her curfew.

She climbed in the cab and fastened her seat belt, unable to hold still while Chad got in. She twisted her hands in her lap and looked straight ahead as she gave directions to her house. The only thing she could think about was how she was going to explain herself if she couldn't sneak in unnoticed by her parents. As they drove along, she became less and less nervous. By the time they turned onto her street, she forgot to be worried about getting into trouble; she could only think about Chad. *Will I ever see him again?* she thought. *Will it be awkward if we run into each other at school in front of our friends?*

Chad walked Holly to her door. He faced her and looked into her eyes. He kissed her forehead and walked away. As she slipped quietly into her house, she realized she didn't even have his phone number, and that for the first time in her life, things were left up to chance. Smiling, Holly tiptoed into her room.

He had decided he didn't want to ruin the fun they had shared that night by asking her any questions. He wasn't sure what would happen on Monday, or if they would even see each other. But he felt content and a sense of accomplishment for the first time in a long while. As he drove home, Chad thought contently that he had known Holly one night, and she had become a friend he would always remember.

Poetry

EARTH REIGNS
BY MAYA NEVAREZ VACA

Earth reigns,
Over all that inhabit its domain.
Harsh waves crashing,
Ruthless winds blowing,
The unforgiving ground shaking,
Many lives are taken
Earth reigns.

With the glorious rays of the sun
Cascading down upon us,
People take this life for granted.
Our mother is weeping,
For the pain that she has endured,
She will makes us pay
Earth reigns.

Tall redwoods stand strong,
Toward the sky they seem everlasting.
The clouds spark our imagination
The world is at peace for a day
Still our mother is angry
At the choices we have made,
Careless, stupid, reckless decisions,
Ones that cannot be taken back.
We *will* pay.
Earth reigns.

Homes collapsing,
Lives shattering,
Five minutes is all it takes.
She reminds us we belong to her,
We survive because of her.
She will find a way to show us,
To punish us like she did that day.
Earth reigns.

The afternoon when the ground shakes,
With uncontrollable force,
Crushing everything,
Leaving nothing,
We remember to be thankful.
Earth reigns.

LIVING SILVER
BY MAYA NEVAREZ VACA

I am long and silver.
Perfect hands move on me
Knowing not how I came to play,
I make music.
Ballads, solos, marches

Many buttons,
Precisely pushed by expert fingertips.
To some I am a wonder,
Making melody with ease
To others, less appreciative,
I am a bore, a noise maker

Nonetheless I am here,
To make music for all to hear.
I am music
I am life,
What keeps her going.

She is my friend, the musician.
She knows me, every part
As I know her through what she plays
"*Costa del sol*"
"Dusk"
"From the Eye of the Storm"
All difficult pieces,

Yet she knows how to move with finesse,
The right position, the right note.

I know her mood by how she treats me.
At times smooth and gentle,
Other times rough and ruthless,
She plays to soothe her troubled mind.
Skilled at her craft,
Uses me everyday.
She never stops
Always playing.

She is mine,
as I am hers.
I am her instrument
I am a flute.

ODE TO A FORGOTTEN PERSON
BY ARIAS JARELLS

Long gone are you now,
Heart aches to find you again.
Struggling to regain you,
You evade me even at this age.
Every time I pass something you've touched,
I feel like I'm falling apart.
I want to meet you.
To ask you questions,
Why did you leave me?
At infancy.
Why do you never come to visit?
In lonely hours,
Or at the times that made me older.
Wanting you to see,
Who I've become.
And the things I plan to do.
Be a part of my future.
To make up for the past.
I know not where you are,
I want to see you
Even if you have forsaken me

THREE WORDS
BY ALYSE BARRIENTOS

That moment
I received your message
My heart stopped
Shock took over

Tears filled my brown eyes
As I read painful words
Shattered my fragile heart
Promises broken

Left without reason
Why you couldn't say
Three words: we're on hold
Confused; should I wait?

Remember, forever and a day?
That's gone now; forget it
Your hoodie is back in my closet
Remains there, until you return
Maybe you'll come back to me
Or maybe you'll move on
Either way, I'll have hope for us
Trying to keep composure

No doubt I miss you
"What ifs" run through my mind
Three words: we're on hold
I'll wait, but not forever.

LIFE
BY MARIA CASTRO

Clickety-Clack
I've just been born
cheerful screams
merciful cries

Tick-Tock
First day of kindergarten
closing doors
screaming children
I'm in it alone

Hipety-Hop
Middle school is here
I'm in utter fear
dirty looks
stepping feet
groping stares

Ding-Dong
time for prom
happy cheers
lustful kisses
Fill me here

Pow.
College.
no boyfriend near
hookups and aspirin doses
stressful nights
and partying sights

Allelujah.
Newlyweds.
love is deep
everything serene
my husband is handsome
Life is perfection

Drip-Drop
I've just been diagnosed with cancer
weakening from the inside
deteriorating from the outside
a divorcee

Beep-Beep-Beep.
no one to live for
no one that cares
Goodbye world thanks
for your happy hours
I'm in it alone.

LITTLE DONNA
BY MARIA CASTRO

Little Donna
odd, I'd look at her
unknowingly
of what was going on
in her head, her heart

Later
I understood
Little Donna
was scarred
raped by her uncle
age thirteen

Hopeless alcoholic mother
shunned her
silenced her words
judging her crazed
ignoring her pleads

Day by day
month by month
her uncle molested
poor Little Donna
she just let it be

Mind control
taught it to ignore
holding all the pain
not knowing what to do
Momma should have listened

he stopped.
too late.
engrossed she scarred
herself: body and arms

she began
drinking, getting high
attempting suicide
trying to escape
disgusted with her reality

all that's left
scars
here's your daughter
you heartless monster
wave to Little Donna

BLADE OF DEATH
BY T. W. ADAMS

I am steel
Birthed from fire
Ready to take life
Sharp and deadly
I can be swung out of control
Or wielded with grace
I contact my brothers in mortal combat
One of us will rest
The other carried on, bloodied

A PLACE FOR ME
BY JENI CHAVEZ

The wet wood fragrance tickles my nose,
Dust surrounds me,
I stifle a sneeze.

Mist and air settles on my coat,
Like a liquid blanket holding me,
Opening my mouth, the breeze dances through,
Causing my lungs to rejoice.

It's so quiet, so quiet I can hear the trees,
I can hear the thump-thump of my own heart,
My vision fades as I begin to feel,
Taste, smell, the world around me.

In this small little house, in this small little tree,
My thoughts run wild like a pen on paper,
Here, in my little bottle at sea.

My little shoebox under the bed,
My own anything, anywhere,
I can be me,
In my small little house, in this small little tree.

JUDGMENT
BY JENI CHAVEZ

They keep their distance,
Lurking in the shadows,
Waiting for him to take a step,
Waiting to start their judgments.
They think they know him,
They don't.
Instead they pick him apart,
Piecing together a monster.
A monster they believe is real,
Boiled and wrapped,
In lies and webs.
But they don't know him,
They don't know anything about him.

NIGHT RAID
BY C. M. FRIDAY

Dust on father's head
Worry in mother's eyes
Crying child of four
And screaming child of six.
The flag of blue, with red lines across
Hung in front of them
Most proud on the wall.
Underground, safe and sound
From the iron that rained
And the explosions that pound.
Radio on, warnings announced
Static overtook.
All is quiet in the foggy town
The carrion birds have departed.
Families emerge to see homes in rubble
The radio, back on,
Proclaimed most valiantly,
"We will defend our island whatever the cost may be...."

LITTLE THINGS
BY C. M. FRIDAY

Crying through infantile lips
Meeting those of same age
Growing more and more
Mind enhancing, body enlarging.
First love, first dance
First kiss, first end.
Sorrow leaves, joy arrives
Ringing of bells
Maiden in white
Crying through infantile lips
Watch them grow
Live, Love, Learn
Bones so brittle, mind slows down
Graying orbs, strands of silver
Resting on bed in black box
Contented smile on cold blue lips
It's really the little things
That matter.

HAPPINESS
BY HAYLIE ERIN HOPPERT

Undefined
You know what it isn't
But how to explain
Beyond words
A mediocre euphoria
A constant jubilation
No translations
No miracle prescription
Pure and natural
A moment in existence

THE FIGHT
BY HAYLIE ERIN HOPPERT

Hand marks scorching skin
Lips trace words of deceit
Flickering eyes
The silhouette of despise
Taste the bountiful hate?
Living lies
You know how to say goodbye
Leave now
Hold your peace
You will burn in your hateful deceit

EXOTIC FLOWER
BY MAREN PETERSON

The exotic flower blooms all year
With no thought for seasons
It blooms for young and old alike
Sometimes for different reasons

It doesn't need seeds, water, or soil
It merely blows by wind and grows
In souls of men, women, and children
Miraculously it blooms and glows

Should this flower ever die out
Then shall men be doomed to die
In bitterness, in envy, in evil
Without a friend to say goodbye

SEED
BY MAREN PETERSON

I start small
Until I push out
Fight to expand

For the first time
I see sunlight
Blinding
Struggle closer

I spread out
Into a disk,
Red, delicate

A human hand
plucks me from
my home

She moves me,
someone smells
my artful aroma

A tinkling laugh,
Bells sounding
I fill with pride,
I caused that

Placed in a
Delicate yellow
Cloud, nestled
Against a cheek
Where I see
The world,
Until slowly,
I die.

HOME AWAY FROM HOME
BY HILARY ALEXANDRIA SPIVEY

My home away from home
Is no home or house at all
Just a place I like to be
Spend my time in peace

Smells of grass, sweet hay, and dew
Morning air crisp on my skin
Afternoon, it changes
The smell of horse sweat, dust and cows
Now raining, mud beneath my boots
Laughter dancing in the wind
Friends at the picnic table

Pizza boxes, hot dogs on a stick
Horses sneak bites of raviolis
Bonfire, BBQ, camp fires all night
Pot luck with friends, dogs, and neighbors

Horses, they nicker
From pens not far off
Night, now close by
We load bales up in trucks
Time to feed, itchy hay
Finds its way in my clothes

Smell of smoke from the fire
A comfort at best
Warms my soul
Fire dances in eyes
The sound of a horse whinny
Carried on the breeze
Up to the night sky
Filled with the moon and stars

DON'T KNOW
BY HILARY ALEXANDRIA SPIVEY

People fear
Whom they don't know
But someone who's feared
Has fears of his own

Small spiders
Eight legs crawling
Or love
Of someone close

No fear of death
He lives life full
One who loves to party
Girls and fun
Escape from reality
Drowns problems in booze and drugs

High school was bad
Strived to improve
Job at sixteen
Survive a little better

No one knew
His athletic appeal
How sports could have been
His release

Because people fear
Whom they don't know
And people they have yet to meet.

BORN TO END
BY ALEXANDRIA TERAN

Born in an instant
Die in a second
Falling from thousands of miles from the sky
Falling faster then ever
Cold
Wet
Swooshing in the wind surrounding me
Getting closer
Surface of the unknown, in my sight
Born in an instant
Die in a second

YOUR NAME
BY JENNA PARMLEY

When I hear your name
So many memories
Spark in my mind.

Stray kittens in the backyard
With silly names
From the minds of two
Second graders.

At the beach,
Pictures in the sand
Sand castles,
Now washed away.

Fourth of July
Sparklers held out like wands.
Running from the flames,
Fireworks paint the sky.

Every time I gain a year
There is ice cream.
Orange sherbet for me,
Something chocolate for you.

In the car, a long trip,
We tell a story never told
Sing a song
We've never heard.

We watch a movie
You laugh when
I jump in fright.
So I laugh too.

Cold winter comes,
We sit in warmth
Toast the New Year

When I hear your name
Memories come.
The leading thought is
My friend.

THE MUSIC BOX
BY JENNA PARMLEY

The music box sits
In the attic alone.
Peeling paint
Glory, now gone.
Dust gathers,
The lonely box
Plays no more.
Silent.

One day a beam
Of light shines bright
From a door opening.
Two little girls smile,
Enter with delight.
The attic, full of wonder,
Offers up its treasures.
Faded dresses are
Ball gowns, beautiful,
New, of worth.
The chipped china
With glasses of crystal
Becomes a queen's
Tea set, beautiful,
New, of worth.

The music box sits,
Still covered in dust.
A small hand brushes
The top clean
The paint shows.
She unlatches the golden
Shining clasp, hoping
The music will play.
Inside a dancer waits
For the song.
Her little tutu, pink,
Waves in the gasp of breath
How beautiful. How perfect.
But wait.
Where is the music?

The little girl finds
A key in the wind.
She turns it,
Three notes play,
Clean, bright, perfect.
She winds it up more and
Lets the song begin.
Tinkling notes find their way.
The dancer begins to spin
Free.

The girls dance.
The dresses sparkle.
The crystal gleams.
The music,
Beautiful, new, of worth.

The girls leave,
Returning to life below.
The dresses fade.
The crystal is boxed.
The music, gone.
The music box sits
In the attic alone,
Its worth hidden
Wrapped up inside
Waiting.

LOST
BY JENNA PARMLEY

The week is new but things are gone.
Lost in the time gone by.
The sun was lost as the clouds moved in,
Rain came pouring down.
A worksheet due was never found.
A necklace was not in my jewelry box.
I couldn't find my favorite shirt,
And my cookie was missing.

In the big picture these don't seem
To hold the worth they did.
What's a day of rain, or two,
To months in the rainy states?
Why worry over a worksheet
Only worth five points?
A necklace is not necessary,
The same goes for my favorite shirt.

I do mourn the cookie's loss,
It was chocolate chip.
Really that is nothing to
Someone going hungry for days.

So if there's always someone else
Whose loss is worse than mine,
Why mention the little things
That are gone?
Everything has a purpose,
Everything has it's time.
Everything is lost at one point,
And everything can be found.

The only loss worth regretting
Is the loss of a friend.
Someone who could be there.
The worst loss is when
They're not.

TIMES AS THIS
BY A. L. STONE

Walking down a trodden road, I hear the leaves beneath my bare feet.
They crackle gently; an orange is being split apart.
Wind blows and stirs the leaves, casting them from the trees.
They break off; a toddler snaps his crayons.
Leaves hit my bare arms with drops of last night's rain still upon them.
They are a dog's nose, rubbing against my flesh.
My head leans back and I breathe in the wintry air, laughing.
The wind wafts into my nostrils; I smell a pen's fresh ink laced with moist
    grass.
My laughter hangs in the air, joining the distant melody of the wind
    chimes to the left.
Twirling around, leaving the world, I submerge into the sound and scent of
    nature.
My spinning ceases, yet the fluid in my head keeps going around.
The dizziness rocking my body; I stand still as though to halt time.
My balance returns to me and I listen for the wind chimes.
A melody like glass shattering enters my ears;
I turn and stop when it comes from the right.
The wind continues to blow, softly now, as I begin to walk home.
Walking down this trodden road, I feel the leaves beneath my bare feet.
They prick harshly; a walk on ice.
During times as this, I forget I am blind.

GAZING THROUGH THE YEARS
BY A. L. STONE

See the hand on the wall,
through the blinds of the window?
It waves goodbye.
Swaying madly, the shadow falls
across the plastered wall, chanting.
Goodbye to all.
Winds blow and uproot the tree.
The hand disappears.
A sorrowful girl gazes out this window,
a soft sigh leaving her as the tree.
Goodbye,
she says to the lost tree.
See the face in the sky,
through the blinds of the window?
It mouths hello.
Soaring calmly, the cloud falls
into the enigmatic path of the wind.
Hello one and all.
Winds blow and break the cloud.
The face disappears.
A sorrowful boy gazes out this window,
a soft sigh breaking as the cloud.
Hello,
he says to the lost cloud.
See the silhouettes in the street,
through the curtains of the church?

They hold hands.
Walking slowly, they rapidly drift
through lost years of shattered time.
Winds blow and go around them.
Clasped hands swing as one.

CONTRIBUTORS' NOTES

T. W. Adams plans to attend College of the Sequoias and California State University, Sacramento, as a European history major. In his free time, he writes music, sings, plays guitar and drums, and listens to Iron Maiden.

Alyse Barrientos, a senior in high school, was born in Hayward, California, and was adopted at two. She lived in San Jose until her freshman year, when she moved to Visalia. She enjoys writing and hopes to pursue a career in journalism.

Jeni Chavez, who prefers to be called Ninja, grew up in Sacramento and is now a senior at El Diamante High School. She is obsessed with the color silver, spends her rainy days playing WoW, and has a cat named Synclaire. Her aspiration is to earn a living in cosmetology and photography.

Maria Castro, an El Diamante High School junior, has participated in a panel with Francisco Jiménez at the 2008 Upward Bound Summer Program. Basketball, reading, and writing are her favorite hobbies, and she plans to attend USC.

C. M. Friday, born in Tulsa, Oklahoma in 1993, has a keen interest in everything artistic, scientific, and philosophical. He has performed in choir concerts and the musicals *Oklahoma* and *The Music Man*. When he had an opportunity to submit works of his own hand to this collection, he almost jumped with excitement.

Haylie Erin Hoppert loves to read and write. Regardless of being a junior in high school, she doesn't know what she wants, but she hopes to end up in Naples, Italy.

Arias Jarrells, a junior at El Diamante High School, is currently writing several series of novels. She says, "Throughout my life, I've bottled up many emotions that have been tearing me up from the inside out. Now is my chance to release them; now is the time to expose the real me."

Maya Nevarez Vaca, a senior at El Diamante High School, has played the flute for eight years. She is a part of the award winning El Diamante Marching Miners and the El Diamante Wind Ensemble, which performed in Carnegie Hall in 2008. After graduating, she plans to become a registered nurse and to continue to write in her free time.

Janet Nichols Lynch is the author of eight books, most recently the young adult novels *Addicted to Her* and a 2010 ALA Quick Pick for Reluctant Young Adult Readers, *Messed Up*. She has an M.M. in Piano and an M.F.A. in Creative Writing. She teaches English at El Diamante High School.

Manuel Magaña was born in Michoacán, Mexico and came to the U.S. when he was two. He lived in L.A. for ten years and moved to the San Joqauin Valley when he was fourteen. A junior at El Diamante High School, he plans to attend California State University, Fresno, and become a veterinarian technician.

Jenna Parmley, a junior in high school, has played the piano for ten years and the flute for six. She hopes to attend a the University of California to pursue a degree in English.

Maren Peterson is an aspiring author. She has played the piano for nine years and intends on continuing. She hopes to pursue a degree in history, and eventually teach it. Her nonfiction piece "My Other Worlds" won first place in the 2010 California Association of Teachers of English (CATE) Creative Writing Contest, high school division, and will be published in *California English*.

Priscilla Portillo was born and raised in L.A., then moved to the Central Valley at age sixteen. She signed up for her school's creative writing class and enjoys it very much. She plans to attend a four-year university.

Chanse Souza is an active person who is always doing something, such as writing, drawing, researching, exercising, or socializing. She wishes to affect the minds and hearts of others with her words. She also created the cover art for this anthology. She would like to open a rescue shelter for reptiles, which are abused, unwanted, or neglected by their owners.

Hilary Alexandria Spivey, a senior, is the president of the El Diamante FFA and has shown market goats and replacement heifers at the Tulare County Fair. She plans to attend California State University, Fresno, and major in diary science.

A. L. Stone is an ambitious musician who has composed over thirty songs and also has had several poems published in junior high literary journals. She plans to major in music at Fresno Pacific University and hopes to publish the two novels she is currently writing.

Alexandria Teran, aka Alex, is a senior at El Diamante High School who enjoys playing soccer. Her main purpose in life is to express herself in new, modern ways through drawing and writing. Alex writes, "Art can be formed in many ways. It all depends on which way you prefer to do it."

Lily Thao is a junior at El Diamnate High School. She is involved in both the dance and the music program at her school. She enjoys drawing while listening to music.